SOCIO-CULTURAL AND ECONOMIC ASPECTS OF GLOBALIZATION

About the Editors

Prof. Krishna Kanta Dhali is Assistant Professor in the Department of History, Gobardanga Hindu College, 24 Parganas (North), West Bengal and also serving as the Secretary of Teacher Council. He has contributed several research articles on Socio-political and Socio-cultural issues which have been published in various reputed journals and edited books. He has published a book entitled *Prachin Biswa Sabhyata: Samajik Gathon O Sanskritik Nidarshan*.

Dr. Tridib Mandal is Assistant Professor in the Department of History, Gobardanga Hindu College, 24 Parganas (North), West Bengal. He is awarded PH.D. for his thesis on 'Swadhinattor kale Banglar Pat-Silper Sangkat O Jatiokaraner Dabi: 1947-1977' by the Rabindra Bharati University, Kolkata, West Bengal. He has contributed several research papers on Socio-political and Socio-cultural issues which have been published in various reputed journals and edited books. He has published a book entitled, *Bangladesh Liberation War: A Retrospect*.

Socio-Cultural and Economic Aspects of Globalization

Edited by

Krishna Kanta Dhali

Tridib Mandal

CONCEPT PUBLISHING COMPANY PVT. LTD.

NEW DELHI - 110 059

ISBN: 978-93-5594-529-7

First Published 2023

Published and Printed by

Concept Publishing Company Pvt. Ltd.
A/15-16, Commercial Block, Mohan Garden
New Delhi-110059 (India)
T: +91-11-4110 1460
E: publishing@conceptpub.com, W: www.conceptpub.com

Cataloging in Publication Data--Courtesy: D.K. Agencies (P) Ltd. <docinfo@dkagencies.com>

Socio-cultural and economic aspects of globalization / edited by Krishna Kanta Dhali, Tridib Mandal.

pages cm
Contributed articles.
Includes bibliographical references and index.
ISBN 9789355945297

1. Globalization—Social aspects—India. 2. Globalization—Economic aspects—India. 3. Globalization—Political aspects—India. 4. Globalization—Environmental aspects—India. I. Dhali, Krishna Kanta, editor. II. Mandal, Tridib, editor.

LCC HN690.Z9G56 2023 | DDC 303.48254 23

FOREWORD

A book is always a welcome sight as it represents the collective wisdom of a whole range of the educated and intellectual existence of ideas in a particular society. According to me, it is a better option than the individual knowledge of an intellectual wizard whose knowledge is refused access by those who do not share any private intimacy with him. I have taken active interest in the collection of articles published under the title *Socio-Cultural and Economic Aspects of Globalization* edited by Sri Krishna Kanta Dhali and Dr. Tridib Mandal, both serving as Assistant Professors in the Department of History. They have been consistent and diligent enough to bring more than eighteen research based articles between two covers. While appreciating their courageous attempt, I confess that only a very well-versed scholar in the relevant field may actually venture to speak on the issues discussed by some eminent scholars of the academia. Globalization is a phenomenal growth in modern life. From the unborn child to the aged, all are within its ambit. The urban, rural and the space of the home or the office, seem to feel its compelling presence and observe its spirit both within and without.

The inclusion of South Asia and its special reference in India deserves special accolade. It is also a rewarding experience to note that several authors have been invited to contribute to this volume from different South Asian countries. They had gathered in the international seminar organized by the college and graced the occasion to a considerable extent. It facilitated the working out of a broader theoretical paradigm within which to explore the question social changes through critical engagement. As the collection concerns both transnational and trans-socio-political and economic aspects of globalization, it suffices to erase any narrow political bias and is not restricted to any singular ideology of an individual nation. Readers of varying academic backgrounds would be keenly observing scholars' debates on a perfect international platform and in the process generate multiplicity of ideas from a cross-cultural orientation. Perhaps the expanse of a single book cannot do justice to the vast repertoire of knowledge that the topic has raised. But, it has at least provided in a brief nutshell the range and intensity of the novelty of ideas that the scholars have professed in their arguments.

Last but not the least, the editors of the present compilation of the book deserve credit for drawing the readers' attention towards multiple socio-political and economical changes entailed by the forces and process of globalization through the nook and corners of the subcontinent and its associations with several countries over the last few decades and the predicaments of social life observed therein. After all, the status of social existence does not remain static through trajectories of history but keeps changing gradually from the colonial to the post-colonial and finally to the post-global context whereby we begin to imagine a post-human condition for ourselves. The present volume tries to grapple with this aspect of globalization having its dominant bearing on Indian culture and ethics and the subsequent changes by which sometimes ethnicity and native heritage is lost. The *pros and cons* of globalization need to be weighed and measured and judged, though not always on the principles of morality, at least on a comparative analysis that refers to the several interventions of elements that in spite of a significantly minor status at times do much to strike at the roots of anthropomorphic knowledge making further investigations into existential aspects for the contemporary cultural matrix.

Dr. Hare Krishna Mandal
Principal
Gobardanga Hindu College

ACKNOWLEDGEMENTS

We would like to express our sincere gratitude to all the contributors who have contributed their valuable and pedagogically profound research papers which will surely lend and insight to the theme of the book. They have contributed to their colossal work in a very short time despite having their busy schedule. We express our gratitude and indebtedness to our respected Principal Dr. Hare Krishna Mandal, Gobardanga Hindu College, who has given his kind consent to pen the foreword of this volume that would surely increase the moral value of the book.

We owe thanks to the Governing Body of the Gobardanga Hindu College, Khantura, North 24 Parganas, West Bengal, and special thanks to Principal Dr. Hare Krishna Mandal, who gave his valuable suggestions and constructive criticism, which helps us to improve work. We would like to thank especially all the Faculty members of all the departments along with the Non-Teaching Staff of the College for their constant support and valuable guidelines throughout.

We would also acknowledge Mr. Ashok K. Mittal of Concept Publishing Company Pvt. Ltd. for his support to release the book in time.

Prof. Krishna Kanta Dhali
Dr. Tridib Mandal

INTRODUCTION

The word "globalization" has been widely promulgated to refer to aspects of development mostly from an economic, socio-political and cultural perspectives. To describe the increasing flow across borders of humankind in general but also of particular individuals, irrespective of their social or ethnic status and labour, capital, goods and services, and the formation of international production networks as represented in multinational enterprises. Many researchers said that with globalization, the processes of "homogenization and heterogenization" occur at the same time. From the political and economic spheres (market economy, small government, democratization) to consumer culture (such as music and movies, products and food culture introduced by multinational agribusinesses, mobile phones), this flow of events that can be observed practically anywhere in the world is entering developing countries. Political globalization is one dimension of a process, that is multidimensional not just economic, historical and transformative. Conceiving of political globalization in evolutionary terms makes it possible to construct a time-table for global politics, and to derive from it an agenda of priority global problems. The following questions will be addressed on that basis: Where in that process are we situated at the present time? What global problems do this analysis point to, and what does it tell us about where we are heading? These are not forecasts but rather elements of an "institutional" framework of orientation for the discussion of the next several decades of global organization.

In the essence of new world globalization, we can connect it with cultural and civilization changes. The terms 'culture' and 'civilization' are found in various ways with the term 'globalization'. The concept of 'culture' occupies a special position in this range. The deep understanding of the phenomenon of civilization came later, in the late nineteenth century when the processes of globalization started to be more and more definite. They were implicit in the theoretical works by Karl Marx, Friedrich Engels, Vladimir Soloviev, Pierre Teilhard de Chardin, Vladimir Vernadsky and Karl Jaspers. In the new era of globalization, people become much more concerned about the uniqueness and particularity of their own culture. Cultural identity provides the global significance of local knowledge and the sense of self, community and nation. Globalization enhances cultural identity and people become much more concerned about the uniqueness of their culture. A concept of civil society that stresses civil society's role in working with the state to achieve more inclusive, democratic polities provides the context for examining the implications for transnational civil society.

The book is a collection of some valuable and insightful research papers presenting the various issues related to *Socio-Cultural and Economical Aspects of Globalization*. The book is divided in four sections.

Section I. Economic Aspects of Globalization

Dr. Tridib Mandal has searched in his article 'Modernization and Special Development for the Jute Industry in the Late Twentieth Century' that the Indian Jute Industry, which is over a century old and has been making significant contributions to the Indian economy, is now passing through a crisis. The Industry does not now enjoy the near-monopoly which it previously did. Many countries have set up jute mills and others are planning to do so. Pakistan has emerged as a major rival to the Indian industry in the world trade in jute goods. Synthetic fibres and substitute methods of packing have also made serious inroads into jute's markets. For the survival and growth of this age-old Indian industry imaginative rethinking is nudged. Discuss various problems of the jute industry, such as industrial sickness, lack of modernization, growing competition from synthetics and default in payment to provident fund and E.S.I. or even wages by the management of some mills, which are here with the idea of indicating the possible means of revitalizing the industry. The State Government and Control Trade Union organizations felt that it was necessary to nationalize the industry and to enforce monopoly procurement of raw jute through Government channels in order to ensure healthy growth of the industry. Stringent steps should also be taken to enforce recovery of arrears of Provident Fund and E.S.I. It was also felt that liberal import of HDPE was not only detrimental to the interest of the jute industry but resulted in outgo of valuable foreign exchange. In course of discussion, the management, the central trade unions and the State Government reached a consensus in respect of the following measures: (i) abolition of the policy of freight equalization by the Government of India; (ii) ban on import of HDPE granules; (iii) ban on substitution of jute goods by synthetics in packaging; and (iv) immediate implementation of the last industrywise settlement in respect of complement of workman (i.e., 90% of the working complement as on 5th May, 1971 should be employed on permanent basis and 20% as special badlis). It was suggested that the Finance Minister, the Industry Minister, the Textile Minister and the Labour Minister of the Government of India should be invited to meeting in Calcutta for a full appreciation of the problems facing the Jute Industry. On September 18, 1986, the Prime Minister announced in Calcutta (now Kolkata) the Creation of two Separate funds — one for modernization of jute mills worth ₹ 150 crore and another for special development fund for jute industry worth ₹ 100 crore for the rehabilitation and modernization of the jute industry.

Dr. Tapan Kumar Roy has shown in his article in 1991, India met with an economic crisis relating to its external debt — the government was notable to make repayments on its borrowings from abroad; foreign exchange reserves, which we generally maintain to import petroleum and other important items, dropped to levels that were not sufficient for even a fortnight. The crisis was further compounded by rising prices of essential goods. All these led the government to introduce a new set of policy measures which changed the direction of our developmental strategies. The Indian experience with globalization and liberalization, although durable and not reversible, has been, during the last decade of reform, somewhat different than most of the other countries. The authorities in India have revealed a preference for an India-specific brand of globalization in which the content, sequence, and timing of policy measures are modulated to contain potential adverse shocks, while maximizing the benefits of cross-border integration. This cautious approach has been guided by the perceived risk-return trade-off. Here we will look at the background of the crisis, measures that the government has adopted and their impact on various sectors of the economy.

Chinmoy Ghosh has tried to develop a concept of business trend analysis with the help of secondary data collected from DION report, CEAMA reports, JP Morgan, Tech Naive, Spark Capital estimates etc. In that particular part of our research we used Ms-excel as well as used statistical software tools to generate a business forecasting model of home appliances production trend to chalk out the development of business and economy of our country in near future. The trend model provides us a path how production of home appliances will boost up the production trend and which will lead to economic development in our country in near future. The Indian consumer durables market has traditionally been a high employ, priority sector. Consumer durables account for more than 40 per cent of end consumer costs in India. Annual turnover of more than INR 500 billion and pays more than INR 150 billion to revenue of Centre and State governments, the sector pays more than 5.5 per cent of IIP. It has been an employment originator — for every direct job, 3 in-direct jobs are shaped. Import demanding sector and second top supplier Urban markets reason for the mainstream share (65% of total revenues) in the consumer durables segment in India, however, upcoming jet growth will originate subsequently in the rural markets (69% rural population).

Shawkat Ali has endeavoured in his article 'Financial Literacy in the Light of Adapting to Globalization and the Cyber World Threats: Meaning and Concept' that the process through which people, ideas and goods spread throughout the world is called Globalization. It promotes more integration and interaction between the world's cultures, governments and economies, which leads to the adoption of open and free trading markets which minimizes trade barriers, removes capital controls and liberalized foreign exchange restrictions. Globalization transform the habits, necessities, opportunities and behaviour of persons and the organization and the different kinds of cyber world threats involved to it. Cyber world threats actually means different kinds of risk involved regarding financial loss, decline to the reputation of any organization from any kind of failure of its information technology systems. Proper implementation and monitoring of appropriate system of financial literacy stimulates different factors of an active citizenship like socially accountable behaviour, decision, support, better mobility and the increase of moral principles, which leads to the improvement of understanding of financial products and concepts of persons and the organization and ultimately lowers the risk involved in the field regarding financial activity. The financial literacy is accredited worldwide as a significant element of the monetary and economic firmness and progress. It cannot be denied that financially literate individuals and organizations contribute positively to an effective function of the financial system.

Section II: Social and Cultural Aspects of Globalization

Kanchana Dodan Godage has talked about the globalization and its impacts on our day-to-day life with her own observations and experiences. Before going to recall her own observations on globalization she would like to see how it has been defined. There are many ways that are used to define the concept of globalization in the social science literature. She would like to quote the prominent sociologist, Anthony Giddens' definition on globalization. For Giddens, globalization means "the intensification of worldwide social relations which link distant localities in such a way that local happenings are shaped by events occurring many miles away and *vice versa*" (Steger, 2009:13). She would say it is a process which tries to intensify the societal relationship from different aspects such as economic, political, cultural, ecological etc. What would be then the means for such intensification? If it is a process or a system, it should have means to operate. To her, those means can be the technology and the techniques.

Kallol Bandyopadhyay in his article "Globalization, Cultural Pluralism and National Identity: Socio-Economic and Historical Perspectives" has rightly pointed out that in the institutionalized academic world in India, the conventional tale of advent of globalization and expansion of its empire started with Manmohan Singh's economic policies and practices; the evolving 'global village' consciousness of the 1970-1980s turned in 1990, into the enormous Indian market, and thereby became the ruling factor in the socio-political lives of Indians and ultimately the unrelenting determinant of their fate. However, in the Bengali consciousness and inexhaustible cultural milieu, this so-called global village consciousness was especially active since the dawn of the connection between Bengali culture and Occidental knowledge. In 1821 after Austria's Chancellor Metternich crushed the uprising in Naples, Rammohan Roy wrote, "I sincerely believe that the revolution of the common people of Naples is our own revolution. The enemies of freedom and friends of tyranny never have and never will achieve final success."

Swapan Kumar Mandal has explicated in his article "Globalization and Folk Art" that Globalization is an international situation that emerged at the end of the twentieth century in which the investment, employment, production and marketing systems of the world reached beyond the physical boundaries and expanded into the inter-state range. As a result, the whole world has become a wider society and various countries are simultaneously participating in the same investment, employment, production and marketing process. It is a mechanism of mutual interaction and interconnection that initiates coordination and interaction between governments, institutions and peoples of different nations. The driving force of this approach is international trade and investment, and its main supporting force is information technology. Environment, culture, political system, economic development and progress and human and social progress. It has a clear effect on everything. On the other hand, Folk art encompasses all kinds of visual art created in the context of folk culture. There are many definitions of folk art, but generally objects have some kind of practical utility rather than merely decorative ones. The makers of folk art are usually trained through a popular tradition rather than a fine tradition of culture. This art created by grouped people who live in the structure of an advanced society but who are separated from the advanced genre of art for geographic or cultural reasons is considered as folk art.

Pinkan Biswas has shown in his article "Socio-Economic Globalization: In Search among Santali People of West Bengal" that indigenous people represent the ancient practices of lifestyle. In modern society, they are deprived from the modernity and also better lifestyles. Due to proper education, they have suffered different problems in daily life. In Indian subcontinent, varieties of indigenous people are found in different places of the country. Santali is constitutionally affiliated language of a group of indigenous people residing basically in West Bengal. Light needs to illuminate, to reach each corner, to enjoy itself by making happiness of the flora in the earth. All living components need light to grow, to be happy and also urge to make happy others. Indigenous people basically are known as tribes who had been following classical lifestyles to survive in this world. Scheduled Tribes (STs) are the constitutionally approved indigenous community of India; they basically are enlisted or scheduled as regards its unique culture and life styles respectively. (Bapi Mishra, B., 2014: 630). In academics, the word 'tribe' is used in anthropology as a conceptual category which refers to both as a 'type of society' (simple, egalitarian) and a 'stage' (devoid of centralized authority) in social evolution. In the Indian context, the anthropologists distinguished tribes as well as related them with the caste society in a continuum. To position 'Tribes' outside the state — and outside Indian society in general — is part of an until now influential anthropological debate on 'tribes' in India, which has explored, in particular, the level of integration of 'tribes' into wider society. It was the eminent Indian anthropologist Andre Béteille, who positioned tribes outside the control of the larger pre-colonial Indian states (Béteille, 1986: 297-318). To counter this, Surajit Sinha has argued that tribes, as a dimension of a 'little tradition', cannot be adequately understood unless they are seen in relation to the 'great tradition' of Indian society (Sinha, 1958: 504-18).

Sasanka Shekhar Roy has pointed out that the world now became a global village which makes distance even shorter, making the cultural and economic relations easier, more efficient and faster. It develops among other activities, actions such as protection and promotion of the human rights, internal interchange of young people, the action of information, spreading and sensitization of public opinion, collaboration in the emergency humanitarian assistance and participation. Globalization can bring countless advantages to young people. They are standing a sharp end of the globalization and be considered key agents of change for globalization, as well as its potential victims. The Youth represent the most dynamic and vibrant segment of the population. India is one of the youngest nations in the World, with about 65 per cent of the population under 35 years of age. The youth in the age group of 15-29 years comprise 27.5 per cent of the population (MYAS, 2019-2020). Now the question is what globalization means to the young people and what is the impact of it has had on their lives?

Soniya Majumder has inquired in her article "Bengal Culture: On Special Reference to the thoughts about Bratachari" that the Globalization is the process of interaction and integration among people, companies and governments worldwide. Globalization has accelerated since the 18th century due to advances in transport and communication technology. The increase in global interaction has caused a growth in international trade and the exchange of ideas and culture. It is primarily an economic process of interaction and integration that is associated with social and cultural aspects. Globalization affects every part of human life. Cultural globalization refers to the transmission of ideas, meaning and values around the world in such a way as to extend and intensify social relation. This process is marked by the common consumption of cultures that have been diffused by the internal, popular culture media and international travel, but there are a number of negative impacts globalization has on cultural diversity, including the influence multinational corporations have on promoting a consumer culture, exploitation of workers and markets and influencing societal values. This promotes a homogeneous set of values and beliefs.

In the same way from the late nineteenth century onwards, middle-class Bengali men displayed major anxieties regarding the declining health of their 'race'. This came at a time when a colonial discourse of 'effeminate' come to the Bengali and Bengalis — especially the English-educated middle class — responded by constructing a counter-discourse that itself was marked by a profound ambivalence. Each individual and each race or nation have their "own rhythm" which is often reflected through their performing arts, but in those days Bengali lost their own specific 'rhythm', they would suffer dire consequences, of becoming extinct. In those days Bengali '*Bhadrolok*' society was accepted a new type of culture which called '*Adhunatan*' or 'Modern' culture. Mainly educated Bengali middle class society mostly accepted this and forgotten their own rhythm.

Biswajit Roy has searched in his article "History of Sanskrit Literature: Impact of Globalization Before and After" that littermate originated in the Vedic period. The Vedic prayers are a reflection of the simple life of that era. Later on, in the age of Upanishads, the feeling of a great power, the complex activities of the Brahmins, the picture of the management of the state and society in religion and memory can be seen. The images of mental transition are also captured in poetry and rhetoric but the existence of history is nowhere to be found. The Sanskrit word '*Itihas*' is interpreted as 'Iti - Ha - As' (1) or 'it was like this', i.e. a faithful account of what was happening then. Here can be any political, social, person-centred description, which will identify the features of the country-time-society of the era. But there no such specific evidence was found. For this, the reasons are as follows: (1) Indifference to the present life and interest in the hereafter. (2) Nomadism or impermanence in life from the age of Vedas. (3) Internal conflict and the constant attacks of foreign enemies. Nationalism did not awakened in India for these reasons and there was no tendency to preserve national history. The passage from one era to another through the chronology and chronology of history, the various features by their mutual comparison and above all the information of progress are found. India's highly advanced mindset is surprisingly silent about this. Among them, researchers have traced the elements of history in puranic literature specially from *Ramayana* and *Mahabharata*. Mahavansa/Mahavamsa written by Mahanama in the fifth century A.D. and Padhabali of Jains. Very little real history has been found from it, excluding imagination and horrible exaggeration.

Section III: Political Aspects of Globalization

Krishna Kanta Dhali has tried to search the socio-economy and political condition of *Dalits* through the impact of Globalization in India. In his article "Socio-economic and Political Upliftment of the Dalits: Globalization and After" is going on to seek that traditionally the so-called

Untouchables or *Dalits* were seen as un-clean in a religious sense and presumed to defile others by their touch or presence. It is understood that they had to live in separate areas, at some distance from others. It is retrieved that they were born for the purpose of serving others; it was believed that they carried out the occupations dealing with ritually defiled materials. According to historical reference, *Dalit* movement was going on since ancient time and it is running till now. In the 19th century, Gopal Baba Walangkar (c. 1840-1900) is generally considered to be the pioneer of the *Dalit* movement, seeking a society in which they were not discriminated against. Another pioneer was Harichand Thakur (1812-1878) with his Matua organization that involved the Namashudra (Chandal) community in the Bengal Presidency. Ambedkar himself believed Walangkar to be the progenitor. Another early social reformer who worked to improve conditions for *Dalits* was Jyotirao Phule (1827-1890). Several *Dalit* groups are rivals and sometimes communal tensions are evident. We know more than 900 *Dalit* sub-castes throughout India, with internal divisions. Emphasizing any one caste threatens what is claimed to be an emerging *Dalit* identity and fostering rivalry among SCs. One thing is clear that it is easier to organize *Dalits* on a caste basis than to fight caste prejudice itself. It may say with an example that Balmikis and Pasis in the 1990s refused to support the BSP, claiming it was a Jatav party but over 80 per cent of *Dalits* from all united *Dalit* castes voted BSP to power in 2007. The impacts of socio-cultural globalization have certainly played an important role in consolidating the BSP in UP and all over India. It would be safe to surmise that many of the SC candidates play a leading role in the SC politics of their respective constituencies all over India. For example, the BSP's progress in Lok Sabha Elections in UP is like the following. BSP increased its votes, in 1985 percentage of votes was 2.6 per cent, in 1989 votes' percentage was 9.5, in 1991 percentage of votes was 11.9, in 1996 votes' percentage was 20.6 and in 1998 votes' percentage was 22. In West Bengal, the political condition of *Dalits* was not better. After Independence, Indian National Congress ruled here but *Dalit* representatives were not there without Pramatha Ranjan Thakur. But there was no minister present in the administrative area in State Assembly Constituency. Many converted *Dalit* Sikhs claim a superior status over the Hindu Raigars, Joatia, Chamars and Ravidasis and sometimes refuse to intermarry with them; they are divided into *Gotras* that regulate their marriage alliances. In Andhra Pradesh, Mala and Madiga were constantly in conflict with each other but as of 2015 Mala and Madiga students work for common *Dalit* cause at University level.

Pankaj Kumar Mandal has explicated in his article the relation between India and South-East Asia. He focused that India has political and cultural links with South-East Asian countries from the ancient period. To constitute stronger relation and to manage India's own economic crisis in 1990s, India initiated Look East approach towards South East Asia. But surprisingly till the end of 2000 A.D. Look East was confined as an economic policy. Later in 2003, a second phase of Look East also declared but the strategic importance between India-ASEAN partnerships got less attention. Although the UPA-2 government from 2012 had shown strategic commitment towards South-East Asian region but after the declaration of Act East Policy by P.M. Narendra Modi, a new shift in strategic partnership has drew much attention. Hence in the present article, the recent status of strategic development between India and ASEAN has been studied. Strategic cooperation is supposed to include all kinds of cooperation. The work is a study of how India is connected with ASEAN states in recent years through cultural diplomatic strategy, defence, security and economy related strategy and cyber technical understanding etc. In this context, it is also shown how India is operating its strategic mechanism with ASEAN organization and individually towards each ASEAN member with bi-lateral, multilateral process through the utilization of soft and hard power initiatives. Before discussing the paper in details let us look into a very brief literature review.

Saswati Das has tried to outline how globalization has affected the state politics of West Bengal and outline its extraterrestrial and international evolution. In her article "Impact of Globalization on the Politics and Culture of the State of West Bengal" has looked for that Globalization is a widely used concept in current world politics. On the one hand, globalization sheds light on the changing nature of the world system, on the other hand, sheds light on the changing nature of functional political and economic relations within the world system. Although the term "World" is very old, the concept of globalization derived from it began to be used in the 1960s. Professor Ronald Robertson is the promoter of the concept of globalization. He formalized and defined the first globalization. He wanted to present the discussion of modernization of sociology in an international context. According to Robertson, globalization as an idea refers to the idea of making the world compressed on the one hand, and the idea of uniting the world on the other. That is, globalization highlights the growing interdependence of trade, military and cultural fields between different countries of the world. But the most important aspect of the concept of globalization is "One world".

West Bengal is no exception where it will be free from the effects of globalization. The impact of globalization on the political and political cultural spheres of West Bengal is far reaching. The use of information technology is the working of political parties in West Bengal in the formulation of public relations policy etc. As a result, the political and cultural form of West Bengal has become a process of IT based governance. The progress or aggression of globalization has hurt the old notion of public administration. The call for a free world market, the unstoppable progress of electronic government has necessitated a change in the old notion of state government management theory. Demands for participatory management and flexible administrative structures have been organized to reinvent the government. Some questions have been raised in the debate as to whether the state public administration should be people-centric or capital-centric or the nature or size of the state government will change etc. The first satellite connections were made in 1970s. Imperialism neo-colonial ever forced house-wives to wear Manchester Clothes, cold water has once again poisoned developing countries. But the disorder that infected the world in the 1990s in the name of globalization is its first symptom of rapid international investment system. Multinational corporations continue to play the most important role as carrier of this disease.

Section IV: Environmental Aspects of Globalization

Kantisree Goswami has looked for the globalization and after effect of mise-en-scene in environment. In his article "Mobile Radiations Causing Loss of Biodiversity: An Overview" has seeked that *globalization* refers to the integration of markets in the global economy, leading to the increased *interconnectedness* of national economies. Markets where globalization is particularly significant include financial markets, such as capital markets, money and credit markets, and insurance markets, commodity markets, including markets for oil, coffee, tin, and gold, and product markets, such as markets for motor vehicles and consumer electronics. The globalization of sports and entertainment is also a feature of the late 20th and early 21st centuries. The term *globalization* became popular in social science in the 1990s. It derives from the word globalize, which refers to the emergence of an international network of economic systems. The term 'globalization' had been used in its economic sense at least as early as 1981, and in other senses since at least as early as 1944. Theodore Levitt is credited with popularizing the term and bringing it into the mainstream business audience in the latter half of the 1980s. Sociologists Martin Albrow and Elizabeth King define globalization as "all those processes by which the people of the world are incorporated into a single world society". Technology is one of the leading factors in the evolution of globalization". Technology has evolved to such an extent that mobile phones are used not only for family or business calls, but they are now a way of living. Mobile phones have become an important tool we can use anytime and anywhere and enable us to do various tasks all at the same time. As a portal for communications, messaging, entertainment and information, mobile phones have become the manifestation of the "digital age".

Priyaranjan Sarkar has searched how to change the climate by the effect of Globalization specially in Sundarbans in West Bengal. He has inquired into in his article "Globalization and Climate Change: A Case Study of Sundarbans" that Sundarbans is the world's largest contiguous mangrove forest and is one of the natural wonders of the world. It was recognized by UNESCO as a Natural Landscape World Heritage site in 1987. The morpho dynamics of "forest-beauty" Sundarbans with endless diversity of vibrating nature is a suitable habitat of world famous luxuriant mangroves and Royal Bengal Tiger. The Sundarban eco-region formed by the Rivers Ganga, Meghna and Brahmaputra is the tidally active lower part of the largest delta in the world consisting of a warren of rivers, creeks, marshes and alluvial floodplain. Morphological zones of this lower part of the delta are the Ganga tidal plain (West) between rivers Hugli and Baleswar, the Ganga tidal plain (East) between rivers Baleswar and Tetulia and the Meghna deltaic plain stretching from river Tetulia until Chittagong coastal plain. At the confluence of the delta and the Bay of Bengal, is the single largest mangrove patch of the world spread across about 10,300 sq.km. of which about 60 per cent is in Bangladesh and the rest in India. This mangrove patch is acknowledged worldwide for its outstanding biodiversity, including the Bengal Tiger, and designated as World Heritage Site in both the countries. This littoral mangrove forest besides serving as the habitat for about 200 tigers, accounting for five per cent of the global population in the wild, also imparts protection from storm surges caused by tropical cyclones by attenuating the impact of cyclones that recur on sub-decadal time scales in the Bay of Bengal.

Nandini Chakraborty has tried to promote the conservation of bio-diversity and build environmental awareness and Bollywood films can play a big role. In her article "Specific Indian Films Based on Global Environmental Issues: Impact on Human Life" has searched that the role of Indian media in promoting environment and sustainability concerns the Indian films have played a revolutionary role in building nationalism and endorsing pro-developmental values; and it continues to be powerfully positioned to do so. Films on environment and wildlife have come a long way in India in the last decade. Celluloid seems to be quite a medium of choice to take the message across. The film making format has also seen a change with many film makers changing over to new ways of storytelling. To promote conservation of bio-diversity and build environmental awareness, Bollywood films can play a big role. If there is little bit of an attempt from mainstream cinema like Bollywood to present issues on environment and wildlife, then it will help us to reach more audiences. Bollywood films should build environmental awareness. Visual media is now recognized as one of the most powerful, engaging and emotive ways to sensitize audiences towards the cause of environmental conservationism. Films illustrate the sheer beauty of the natural world, inspiring an entire generation of conservationists across the globe.

It is not necessary that all such films need to be hard-hitting and serious. Film industry can even make nature films for the masses with pure entertainment value, with a message — save the earth. If more people are able to relate to nature and environment through an entertaining film, even then the purpose is served. Pointing out that Indian documentary makers like Mike Pandey have been successful in promoting the cause through his films. But India needs more such efforts. Documenting the massacre of whale sharks on the Indian coast, "Shores of Silence", made in 2000 by Pandey, became a landmark film after it was successful in moving the Indian Government into bringing in legislation and ban the killing of whale sharks. Safeguarding the environment is one of the major challenges faced by most of the major countries in the world. Though there are numerous laws drafted by the government in this regard, it lags in the efficient implementation of it. It is high time that government has to chalk out the plan to educate common man about the implications of deteriorating environment and his/her role in safeguarding it.

Prof. Krishna Kanta Dhali
Dr. Tridib Mandal

CONTENTS

Section – III
Political Aspects of Globalization

Section – IV
Environmental Aspects of Globalization

LIST OF CONTRIBUTORS

Biswajit Roy, State Aided College Teacher (SACT), Department of Sanskrit, Saheed Nurul Islam Mahavidyalaya, North 24 Parganas, West Bengal. *Email: biswajitroy94756046@gmail.com*

Chinmoy Ghosh, Research Scholar, Makaut Faculty of Commerce, East Calcutta Girls' College, Lake Town, Kolkata, West Bengal. *Email: chin.lord@gmail.com*

Dr. Kallol Bandyopadhyay, Associate Professor, Department of History, Sri Chaitanya College, Habra, North 24 Parganas, West Bengal. *Email: kallolbandyopadhyay01@gmail.com*

Kanchana Dodan Godage, Senior Lecturer (On Contract), Department of Social Studies, the Open University of Sri Lanka, Sri Lanka. *Email: dgkanchana84@gmail.com*

Kantisree Goswami, Assistant Professor in Zoology, Charuchandra College, 22 Lake Road, Kolkata-29, West Bengal. *Email: kantisreegoswami@gmail.com*

Krishna Kanta Dhali, Assistant Professor, Department of History, Gobardanga Hindu College, Khantura, North 24 Parganas, West Bengal. *Email: kkdhali75@gmail.com*

Nandini Chakraborty, Assistant Professor, Department of Journalism and Mass Communication, Mrinalini Datta Mahavidyapith, Birati, West Bengal. *Email: chakrabortynandini009@gmail.com*

Dr. Pankaj Kumar Mandal, Assistant Professor, Department of History, Barrackpore Rastraguru Surendranath College, Barrackpore, North 24 Parganas, West Bengal. *Email: pankajmandalbrsc@gmail.com*

Pinkan Biswas, State Aided College Teacher (SACT), Gobardanga Hindu College, Khantura, North 24 Parganas, West Bengal. *Email: pinkanbiswas78@gmail.com*

Priyaranjan Sarkar, Assistant Professor, Department of History, Khalisani Mahavidyalaya, Chandannagar, Hooghly, West Bengal. *Email: priya.hist@gmail.com*

Saswati Das, State Aided College Teacher (SACT), Department of Political Science, Banipur Mahila Mahavidyalaya, Habra, West Bengal. *Email: saswatidas211@gmail.com*

Shashanka Sekhar Roy, Assistant Professor in History, Saheed Nural Islam Mahavidyalaya, North 24 Parganas, West Bengal. *Email: profssroy35@gmail.com*

Shawkat Ali, Assistant Professor, Department of Commerce, Gobardanga Hindu College and A Research Scholar of West Bengal State University, North 24 Parganas, West Bengal. *Email: shawkatali 00001@gmail.com*

Dr. Soniya Majumder, Research Scholar of Rabindra Bharati University, Kolkata, West Bengal. *Email: iamsoniyamajumder1982@gmail.com*

Swapan Kumar Mandal, Assistant Professor, Department of History, Dinabandhu Mahavidyalaya, Bongaon, North 24 Parganas, West Bengal. *Email: skm.hist@gmail.com*

Dr. Tapan Kumar Roy, Assistant Professor, Department of Economics, Mrinalini Datta Mahavidyapith, Birati, West Bengal. *Email: tkreco68@gmail.com*

Dr. Tridib Mandal, Assistant Professor, Department of History, Gobardanga Hindu College, Khantura, North 24 Parganas, West Bengal. *Email: tridibmandalghc@gmail.com*

SECTION – I

Economic Aspects of Globalization

1

Modernization and Special Development for the Jute Industry in the Late Twentieth Century

Tridib Mandal

The Indian Jute Industry, which is over a century old and has been making significant contributions to the Indian economy, is now passing through a crisis. The Industry does not now enjoy the near-monopoly which it previously did. Many countries have set up jute mills and others are planning to do so. Pakistan has emerged as a major rival to the Indian industry in the world trade in jute goods. Synthetic fibres and substitute methods of packing have also made serious inroads into jute's markets. For the survival and growth of this age-old Indian industry imaginative rethinking is nudged. Discuss various problems of the jute industry, such as industrial sickness, lack of modernization, growing competition from synthetics and default in payment to provident fund and E.S.I. or even wages by the management of some mills, which are here with the idea of indicating the possible means of revitalizing the industry.

The State Government and Central trade union organizations felt that it was necessary to nationalize the industry and to enforce monopoly procurement of raw jute through Government channels in order to ensure healthy growth of the industry. Stringent steps should also be taken to enforce recovery of arrears of Provident Fund and E.S.I. It was also felt that liberal import of HDPE was not only detrimental to the interest of the jute industry but resulted in outgo of valuable foreign exchange. In course of discussion, the management, the central trade unions and the State Government reached a consensus in respect of the following measures[1]: (i) abolition of the policy of freight equalization by the Government of India; (ii) ban on import of HDPE granules; (iii) ban on substitution of jute goods by synthetics in packaging; and (iv) immediate implementation of the last industry-wise settlement in respect of complement of workman (i.e. 90% of the working complement as on 5th May, 1971 should be employed on permanent basis and 20% as special *badlis*). It was suggested that the Finance Minister, the Industry Minister, the Textile Minister and the Labour Minister of the Government of India should be invited to meeting in Calcutta for a full appreciation of the problems facing the Jute Industry.

On September 18, 1986, the Prime Minister announced in Calcutta the Creation of two Separate Funds — one for modernization of jute mills worth ₹ 150 crore and another for Special Development Fund for jute industry worth ₹ 100 crore for the rehabilitation and modernization of the jute industry.[2]

Jute Modernization Fund

The Jute Modernization Fund has been established under the auspices of Industrial Finance Corporation of India. IFCI along with IRBI will arrange for flow of funds to the jute mills for undertaking modernization. Under the scheme up to 80 per cent of the debt portion will be given at concessional rate of interest of 11.5 per cent. In respect of 20 per cent of the promoter's contribution further concessional loan at the rate of 6 per cent will be available from IFCI/IRBI. To enable the Financial Institutions to lend at soft terms, the Government of India will provide interest subsidy to them from out of the budget of the Ministry of Textiles. The scheme has become operative from 1st November, 1986 and will remain valid for the present two years. In order to enable the mills to embark upon the programme of modernization, the Government of India has also issued a notification exempting certain specific items of jute textile machinery from the purview of customs duty.[3]

A monitoring committee has been set up under the chairmanship of Secretary, Ministry of Textiles. It includes Secretary, Department of Commerce and Industry, Government of West Bengal as the State Government nominee. The Committee has met four times till April 1987. It was noted that whereas 39 jute mills had collected application forms, only 8 mills had submitted their application for assistance.[4] The general feeling that emerged out of the meetings of the Committee is that modernization alone was not enough and that it was necessary to undertake rehabilitation along with modernization.

One of the issues that is raised in regard to modernization of jute industry is the need for redeployment and rationalization of labour force. An analysis of the employment situation, however, shows that the labour force in some of the mills is high because superannuated workers continued in employment as they had not been paid their retirement benefits. The Chairman, IJMA in fact mentioned at the seminar held on December 22, 1986 that there would be no need for retrenchment for undertaking modernization programme.[5] However, in a written submission to the State Government, the IJMA had stated that modernization would entail retrenchment of 35 per cent of the workforce. In that event alternative employment opportunities should be created by the industry through diversification of their existing product lines and investment in new Industrial units. Besides schemes should be formulated for training and financial assistance to promote self-employment.

Special Development Fund

The Ministry of Textiles have identified schemes for the Special Jute Development Fund and have constituted working Groups to suggest the modalities for the schemes. The schemes relate to development of agriculture, strengthening of procurement of machinery, product diversification and R.D. Support as well as benefits of workers in the jute industry. The deployment of special Development Fund for these purposes has been made by the Government of India in their Memo No. 9/26/86 jute dated 20.1.1987.[6] It was pointed out by the State Labour Secretary at the meeting of the working group on schemes for benefit of workers that one of the primary objectives of the Special Development Fund should be reopening and restructuring of jute industry. The purpose of creating the fund would be defeated if the operation of the schemes was limited to mills which were going in the Government of India was to assist these mills which were financially viable to undertake modernization programme and to pave way to closure of unviable mills through grant of terminal benefits to workers. The State Governments were opposed to closure of mills. There were a number of mills which were technologically sound but had closed down because of financial problems. These should be revived through replacement of management and restructuring of capital. The Government of India should also consider participation in equity capital of closed units particularly in cases where the State Governments came forward with financial assistance by way of Loan and Equity.

In the Sixth Five Year Plan, 1980-85, the Central Government has laid a major emphasis on the production and export of jute goods. The target is for production of 15 lakh tonnes of jute goods in 1984-85, against production of 13.37 lakh tonnes in 1979-80. As regards export of jute goods, the target is to increase annual export to the level of ₹ 345 crore in 1984-85, from the level of ₹ 284 crore in 1979-80.[7] At present, there are 72 jute mills in India with an approximate installed capacity of 14 lakh tonnes, of these 56 mills are located in West Bengal which accounts for about 90 per cent of all India production of jute goods.[8]

After 1976, there has been a progressive increase in the average daily number of workers employed in jute mills in West Bengal. The average daily number of workers employed in Jute mills in West Bengal increased to 2.38 lakh in 1979 from 2.30 lakh in 1977 and 2.33 lakh in 1978.[9] During the year 1980-81, the all India production of jute goods stood at 14.06 lakh tonnes against production of 13.49 lakh tonnes in 1979-80. There was an improvement in production of all categories of jute goods, expected carpet backing, during the year 1980-81. The decline in the output of carpet backing cloth was attributable to slump in export demand. The substantial improvement in production during the year was also attributable to the optimum utilization of the capacity as a result of comfortable supply of raw materials at much cheaper prices and generally improved working conditions in the mills. The industry employed the idle manufacturing capacity for carpet backing for production of hessian and sacking and these items being heavier in weight, resulted in an impressive increase in the volume of production on the basis of tonnage weight. Besides, installation of standby diesel generating sets by most of the jute mills have also helped higher unitization of installed capacity. During the year 1981-82, 13 jute mills in West Bengal have been under closure resulting in decline in production of jute goods during the year.[10] Table 1.1 gives category-wise production figures of jute goods during the years from 1977-78 to 1980-81.[11]

Table 1.1: Production of Jute Goods (in thousand tonnes)

Year	*Hessian*	*Sacking*	*Carpet Backing*	*Others*	*Total*
1977-78	361.1	528.7	136.5	151.8	1178.1
1978-99	279.2	511.0	112.9	143.9	1047.0
1979-80	374.4	665.7	131.1	178.0	1349.2
1980-81	394.6	745.7	73.8	190.0	1406.1

Internal Consumption

During the year 1980-81, internal consumption of jute goods stood at

921.8 thousand tonnes, against 824.3 thousand tonnes during the year 1979-80. The share of Internal consumption to the total production of jute goods also increased to 66.3 per cent in 1980-81 from 61.6 per cent in 1979-80, 66.76 per cent in 1978-79 and 62.8 per cent in 1976-77. The large domestic off take of sacking helped jute mills to maintain their sacking capacity utilization at the optimum level despite a heavy slump on the export front.[12] Table 1.2 shows category-wise internal consumption of jute goods during the last four years.[13]

Table 1.2: Internal Consumption of Jute Goods (in thousand tonnes)

Year	*Hessian*	*Sacking*	*Carpet Backing*	*Others*	*Total*
1977-78	95.8	441.3	—	109.7	646.8
1978-99	98.7	480.7	—	119.3	698.7
1979-80	98.4	583.0	—	142.9	824.3
1980-81	121.2	646.9	—	153.7	921.8

Export of Jute Goods

Export of jute goods in the year 1980-81, both in terms of quantity and value, substantially declined. In terms of quantity, it declined to 4.4 lakh tonnes in 1980-81 from 4.9 lakh tonnes in 1979-80. In terms of value, it declined to ₹ 326.41 crore in 1980-81, from ₹ 334.57 crore in 1979-80. In 1981-82 (up to December 1981) also, the export of jute goods was sluggish (₹ 180.35 crore).[14] Following the imposition of export duty at the rate of ₹ 1000 per tonne on all shipments of hessian cloth and bags on and from 18th February, 1980 for mopping up windfall profits being earned by the industry, market situation in hessian underwent a radical change which brought about a decline in fresh export sales, steep fall in prices and some accumulation of unsold inventory with mill. On a review of the situation, the Government abolished the export duty on this item with effect from 9th September, 1980. In the export markets, competition from Synthetics and Bangladesh continued to be very acute.

Purchase of Raw Jute

During the year 1980-81, the Jute Corporation of India was able to procure 10.62 lakh bales (180 kg) of jute through its direct purchasing centres and cooperatives of which 4.71 lakh bales of raw jute were procured from West Bengal (3.25 lakh bales) through direct purchasing centres of the corporation and 1.46 lakh bales through cooperatives. During the year 1981-82 (up to 31st January, 1982), the Corporation procured 17.48 lakh bales of raw jute of which 10.62 lakh bales were from West Bengal. It may be mentioned here that during the corresponding period in 1980-81, the Corporation could procure only 9.82 lakh bales of raw jute of which 4.62 lakh bales were procured from West Bengal.[15]

Reopening of Closed Jute Mills

By an ordinance promulgated on 27.4.1980 (which was replaced subsequently by an Act) Government nationalized the National Company, the biggest jute mill in the country. A statutory organization, namely, National Jute Manufacturer's Corporation was also set up by the Government of India in order to manage this unit. With a view to securing proper management, five other taken over units, namely Alexandra, Kinnison, Khardah and Union Jute Mills in West Bengal and RBHM Jute Mills in Bihar, were nationalized by the Government on 21-12-1980 under the Jute Companies (Nationalization) Act, 1980. An outlay of ₹ 5.63 crore has been provided in the Central Sixth Five Year Plan for rehabilitation and modernization of these mills.[16]

Handbook and Directory

The Handbook and Directory of Indian Jute Industry is primarily designed to serve as a guide to buyers of jute goods overseas. It contains a comprehensive list of jute manufactures — Standard goods and specialities of different constructions plus a buyer's guide and a section giving the numerous uses of the fabric. The latest information on research, evolution of standard specifications and specific and new uses of jute goods has also been included.[17] Publishing this Handbook and Directory, the Indian Jute Mills Association has attempted to meet a long felt need in the field of international trade in jute textiles. Over 450 different items of jute manufactures have been listed and a buyer's guide has been provided. This book also gives standard specifications of jute cloth and bags and describes the quality control and pre-shipment inspection measures adopted by the jute industry.[18]

New Products Ideas

Universal Moisture Meter — A universal moisture meter has been developed by Oriental Science Apparatus Workshop, Ambala in collaboration with CSIO, Chandigarh. The instrument can be used to measure the moisture content of foodgrains — Seeds, organic and inorganic materials. It works on the principle that the electrical resistance of a sample of a specified weight or volume compressed to a particular pressure varies with temperature and moisture content. Moisture reading can be obtained accurately and quickly in the instrument. The meter is portable, self-contained and operates with 1.5 volt cells. It gives direct reading for moisture contents of 10 to 30 per cent.[19]

New Uses of Jute

Reinforced plastic industry is a promising field for new uses of Jute. Jute cloth represents low-cost bulk. Used as a 'Sandwich' with a layer of glass/fibre on either side, it can provide an economic solution to problems involving structural rigidity where thickness is more important than ultimate strength. According to a U.K. report, decorative jute fabrics are very much in the news and much attention has been given the problem of fastness to light and to rubbing. Both these qualities may be improved considerably by special treatments and improved processing and jute fabrics can now give a reasonable performance in many situations.[20] Plastic coated fabrics are finding substantial industrial outlets and the possibilities of using jute as a substrate material are arousing increasing interest. In this area, jute has to compete with other textiles and various parametric characteristics must be borne in mind in selecting end-uses. With a suitable contraction coated jute fabrics should compare favourably in performance and in cost.[21]

Polyethylene Net for Fabric Lamination

A high density polyethylene net has been used as the bonding material in a fabric laminating process. The process consists of feeding a thin Polyethylene net, Sandwiched between the face and the backing fabrics, through a heating zone. The net gets disrupted in the heating zone, leaving a regularly patterned application of polyethylene which effectively spot-welds two fabrics. According to the report, the process, which is a simple, rapid and clean method of fabric lamination, has created interest because of its advantage over the conventional wet adhesive fabric laminating.[22]

Colourful Jute Fabrics for Home and Industry

Demand for decorative well hessians and furnishing fabrics, particularly in the West, is on the increase in line with the current trend in interior decoration. In the context of this expansion of market for coloured jute cloth, the IJMA bleaching/dyeing process developed last year, which imparts a large degree of colour fastness to the dyed fabric, has assumed great significances.[23]

Prototype Lustre Meter

Lustre is well known quality characteristic of raw jute. A more lustrous fibre is generally associated with higher strength. A rapid method of measuring the lustre property should, therefore, be useful for correlating and evaluating the intrinsic strength of the fibre. Indian Jute Industries Research Association has developed a prototype lustre meter for grading raw jute quality. The measurement of lustre on this model is simple and rapid. Bundles of fibre to be tested are placed on the test plate of the instrument, containing a small aperture and the corresponding lustre reading is obtained directly on the calibrated scale of the meter. The test does not involve weighing of the sample or calculation of results as required in the usual methods of measuring fibre strength.[24] A stabilized beam of light is focused into the narrow spot which emerges through the small aperture in the test plate. When the sample under test is placed on the slit, a part of this light gets reflected from the sample, depending on the lustre of the fibre; the intensity of this specularly reflected beam of light is then measured with the help of a photocell device.

From the results of tests on a number of samples of jute it has been found that the lustre meter reading is well correlated with the tensite strength of the fibre obtained both by the flat bundle and the ballistic work of rupture methods. Work is in progress at IJIRA on the development of a finished model corresponding to the prototype.[25]

A New Shrink-proofing Process

A continuous process for shrink proofing wool to give machine washable textiles has been developed by the Commonwealth Scientific and Industrial Research Organization, Australia. Wool is first treated with an extremely weak solution of chlorine which is subsequently neutralized. Thereafter, it passes through a week solution of resin and is subsequently dried and spun in the conventional manner. The process is a continuous one and has the advantage of being applied at the "top stage, a term denoting the combed form of a mass of fibres prior to spinning."[26]

Jute-backed Carpets for Office Floors

Double jute-backed tufted carpet cemented directly to basic flooring in the general office area of a large newly constructed commercial building. Installed without underpadding, this technique permits easy movement on carpeting of carts, floor trucks and caster mounted furniture with standard wheels of casters.[27]

Improved the Woolpack

Mill's finishing departments, assisted by the quality control personnel, see to it that no woolpack is passed for bundling and packing until it is thoroughly inspected and vacuum cleaned. The chief object of this exercise is to eliminate any possibility of consumer complaint on account of loose fibre and yarn inside the pack.[28] At every stage of processing, the production quality of the new light weight woolpack is rigorously controlled.

Therefore, the main attractions of the new light weight woolpack from India for wool growers and tradets are its improved appearance, reduced fibre shedding, lighter weight, improved quality of fibre, regular and less hairy yarn, improved geometry, high strength, less strength variability, high dimensional stability.

Jute Netting for Erosion Control

Jute netting for soil conservation is most effective in situations where (1) the soil is highly erodible, (2) the quantity of runoff is very high, and (3) it takes a long time for vegetation to grow thereby letting the implanted seeds and sprigs to get dislodged or washed away before they have had the time to take root.[29]

There are other methods of erosion control, but the use of jute netting is particularly advantageous because (1) the method is economical, (2) the jute netting is easy to apply, (3) it is immediate acting, (4) the netting decomposes and fertilizes the soil as vegetation proceeds, and (5) it does not limit the choice of vegetation.[30]

India Assures Quality in Jute Goods

The Indian Jute industry's production is covered by the quality standards of the Indian Standards Institution (ISI). ISI marks on bales are an assurance of the quality of the goods packed. Jute goods covered by ISI standards are not cleared by customs for shipment if packed in bales without ISI marks.[31] The WHY of standards, WHAT they relay mean and HOW they are enforced.[32]

WHY — In the past the quality of jute goods was guaranteed at the time of shipment to be Fair Average Calcutta Quality (FACQ) served the customers well for nearly a century. However, the world buyers, of late, have become increasingly discriminating while the manufacturing industry has also been steadily branching out into new sophisticated lines of production. In this changed context, FACQ was considered inadequate. For better buyer-seller rapport quality characteristics of jute goods needed defining specifically. The industry, therefore, extended its full cooperation to the Indian Standards Institute for formulation of Precise Specifications for its products.

WHAT — The Standards describe the specific quality characteristics of hessian (burlap), Sacking, Jute bagging for cotton bale covering and bags in measurable units.

They specify those quality characteristics which are important for the consumer, namely dimensions, weight, oil and water content, breaking load and mode of packaging.

HOW — The enforcement of standards has entailed:

(i) The adoption of modern concepts of industrial engineering and quality control;

(ii) The implementation of an approved schedule of sampling and test methods;

(iii) A complete reorientation of the methods of production, supervision, operation and maintenance in the mills, involving training of personnel in standards, standardization and operation; and

(iv) The adoption of a certification marks scheme under the Export (Quality Control & Inspection) Act, which has made pre-shipment inspection and quality control in the Jute industry a statutory obligation.

New Machines for Product Diversification

To diversify production as well as to bring down the unit cost of products, the jute industry has soon to modernize over a large area of operation. A ₹ 500 million industry wide programme has already been drawn up (*Jute Chronicle, 1969*, Vol. 4, No. 1). Covering nearby every section of mill processing — batching, softening and carding, drawing, spinning, winding, beaming and weaving.

As a modest start to modernization essential for the production of sophisticated articles from jute, quite a few mills are installing new plants and machinery, including these for bleaching and dyeing and for the manufacture of laminated products.[33] Photographs of some modern machines in the middle twentieth century —

Fig. 1.1: Modern Sizing Machine with Automatic Control for Moisture and Tension.

Fig. 1.2: A Modern Spinning Frame.

Fig. 1.3: Fully Automatic Looms for Manufacture of the Fine Fabric.

Cost Reduction

Cost conditions, high or low, are often built into the very structure of an organization comprising both technological and managerial features. Any cost reduction programme will, therefore, start with a critical probe of these conditions. Likewise, long-term capital project planning will be necessary to cope with the increasingly difficult conditions in the 1970s with spiralling wages, slackening overseas demand, growing competition from other countries and from synthetic fibres.[34] Serious consideration should be given to the long range effect on cost of the following sections of processing equipment:[35]

(i) Improved carding machines which can produce uniform fibres from low-grade jute.
(ii) Improved equipment for processing cuttings and wastes.
(iii) Introduction of auto-levelling drawing frames.
(iv) High speed automatic winding machine.
(v) Individually driven under pick loom with positive uptake, positive let off, warp stop and weft stop motions and other devices like cope changers along with arrangements at the temples for producing clean selvedge.
(vi) Mechanical handling of process material all along the line.

By and large, the industry is conscious of the need for keeping costs down to the minimum and both long and short-term measures of cost reduction have been receiving the attention of persons at the helm of affairs.

Finally, the IJMA stated at the meeting (organized by the State Government at Great Eastern Hotel on November 14, 1986) that the use of Synthetic bags should be banned; alternatively the jute bags should be banned; alternatively the jute mills should be allowed to manufacture blended products (85% jute and 15% synthetics) for which there was market. According to them along with modernization of the mills it might be necessary to undertake rationalization of labour force and retrenchment without tears. The representatives of the Central Trade Unions, on the other hand stated that modernization of the industry should be based on proper manpower planning. A scheme which provided for retrenchment of workers would be totally unacceptable to them. They also reiterated their demand for nationalization of the industry, monopoly purchase of raw jute, ban on import of HDPE granules, immediate clearance of P.F. and E.S.I. dues.[36]

Likewise, the Minister of State for Labour, Government of West Bengal stated that a modernization scheme for the industry should provide full employment to the existing labour force and there should not be any retrenchment. He expected that the Central Government would issue necessary directives immediately to the management for payment of their dues to Provident Fund and E.S.I. which had been rising alarmingly. The Labour Minister further stated that the State Government was firmly of the view that nationalization of the industry and monopoly purchase of raw jute through Government channels were necessary for saving the industry.[37] In the same time, the Chief Minister, West Bengal, who inaugurated the seminar (seminar on Rehabilitation and Modernization of Jute Industry was organized in Great Eastern Hotel, Calcutta on 22nd December, 1986, by Jute Manufacturers Development Council) stated that the State Government considered three steps, namely nationalization of jute industry, monopoly procurement of raw jute and a complete ban on the import of synthetic granules as it is absolutely necessary for revitalization of the jute industry.[38]

Under the circumstances, the Union Labour Minister stated that the Central Government did not think that nationalization would serve the interest of the industry. There should be understanding and co-operation between the management and the unions if the problems of the industry were to be solved. He stated that process of modernization should not be at the cost of labour. There should be training and redeployment of labour to the extent possible though retrenchment through golden handshake might become unavoidable in some cases. He assured that the Central Government would see that arrear, P.F., E.S.I. and gratuity were paid by the employers and if necessary, amendments to the existing Acts would be made.[39]

A proposal of modernization of jute mills is being contemplated by the Central Government. But neither the State Government nor the Central Trade Unions have detailed information with regard to such modernization scheme. The State Government has serious apprehension with regard to such modernization scheme if it is not supplemented by diversification as well as expansion of the mills as modernization will definitely lead to shrinkage of job opportunities in the jute industry. Any modernization scheme should be done with proper manpower planning so that it does not lead to increasing unemployment. Serious imbalance may occur if such modernization scheme is carried out only in selected units and not in the industry as a whole. Out of the fund made available for such modernization, a sizeable portion should be earmarked for training and re-deployment of workers and payment of arrear, P.F. and E.S.I. dues in full. For monitoring allocation of such funds, a high level Committee should be formed with suitable representation from the State Government, central trade unions, management representatives, Government of India. The Committee should also frame suitable guidelines for the jute industry.

NOTES

1. *Labour in West Bengal — 1986*, Department of Labour, Government of West Bengal, p. 28.
2. *Ibid.*
3. *Ibid.*, p. 29.
4. *Ibid.*
5. *Ibid.*
6. *Ibid.*
7. *A Review of Industrial Growth in West Bengal*, Commerce and Industries Department, Government of W.B., p. 89.
8. *Ibid.*
9. *Ibid.*
10. *Ibid.*, p. 90.
11. Office of the Jute Commissioner, Calcutta.
12. *A Review of Industrial Growth in West Bengal*, Secretariat Library, p. 90.
13. *Ibid.*
14. *Ibid.*, p. 91.
15. *Ibid.*, p. 92.

16. *Ibid.*, p. 93.
17. *Jute Chronicle*, Vol. 2, No. 1, January-February, 1967.
18. *Ibid.*
19. "New Products Ideas Services", *Jute Chronicle*, Vol. 2, No. 1, p. 64.
20. *Ibid.*
21. *Ibid.*
22. *Ibid.*
23. *Ibid.*, p. 12.
24. *Ibid.*, p. 14.
25. *Ibid.*
26. *Ibid.*
27. *Jute Chronicle*, Vol. 3, No. 1, 1968 (January-February), p. 83.
28. *Jute Chronicle*, Vol. 2, No. 1, 1967 (January-February), p. 63.
29. *Ibid.*, p. 83.
30. *Ibid.*
31. *Jute Chronicle*, Vol. 3, No. 1, 1968 (January-February), p. 81.
32. *Ibid.*, p. 82.
33. *Jute Chronicle*, Vol. 4, No. 1, 1969, p. 64.
34. N.P. Mukherjee, "Cost Reduction in the Jute Industry", *Jute Chronicle*, 1969, p. 70.
35. *Ibid.*
36. *Problems in Jute Industry: Labour in West Bengal*, Government of West Bengal, 1986, p. 28.
37. *Ibid.*
38. *Ibid.*
39. *Ibid.*

2

Globalization of Indian Economy

Tapan Kumar Roy

Introduction

In 1991, India met with an economic crisis relating to its external debt — the government was notable to make repayments on its borrowings from abroad; foreign exchange reserves, which we generally maintain to import petroleum and other important items, dropped to levels that were not sufficient for even a fortnight. The crisis was further compounded by rising prices of essential goods. All these led the government to introduce a new set of policy measures which changed the direction of our developmental strategies. The Indian experience with globalization and liberalization, although durable and not reversible, has been, during the last decade of reform, somewhat different than most of the other countries.

The authorities in India have revealed a preference for an India-specific brand of globalization in which the content, sequence, and timing of policy measures are modulated to contain potential adverse shocks, while maximizing the benefits of cross-border integration. This cautious approach has been guided by the perceived risk-return trade-off. Here we will look at the background of the crisis, measures that the government has adopted and their impact on various sectors of the economy.

Background

The origin of the financial crisis can be traced from the inefficient management of the Indian economy in the 1980s. We know that for implementing various policies and its general administration, the government generates funds from various sources such as taxation, running of public sector enterprises etc. When expenditure is more than income, the government borrows to finance the deficit from banks and also from people within the country and from international financial institutions. When we import goods like petroleum, we pay in dollars which we earn from our exports. Development policies required that even though the revenues were very low, the government had to overshoot its revenue to meet challenges like unemployment, poverty and population explosion. The continued spending on development programmes of the government did not generate additional revenue. Moreover, the government was not able to generate sufficiently from internal sources such as taxation. When the government was spending a large share of its income on areas which do not provide immediate returns such as the social sector and defence, there was a need to utilize the rest of its revenue in a highly efficient manner. The income from public sector undertakings was also not very high to meet the growing expenditure. At times, our foreign exchange, borrowed from other countries and international financial institutions, was spent on meeting consumption needs. Neither was an attempt made to reduce such profligate spending nor sufficient attention was given to boost exports to pay for the growing imports. In the late 1980s, government expenditure began to exceed its revenue by such large margins that meeting the expenditure through borrowings became unsustainable. Prices of many essential goods rose sharply. Imports grew at a very high rate without matching growth of exports. As pointed out earlier, foreign exchange reserves declined to a level that was not adequate to finance imports for more than two weeks. There was also no sufficient foreign exchange to pay the interest that needed to be paid to international lenders. Also no country or international funder was willing to lend to India. India approached the International Bank for Reconstruction and Development (IBRD), popularly known as World Bank and the International Monetary Fund (IMF), and received $7 billion as loan to manage the crisis. For availing the loan, these international agencies expected India to liberalize and open up the economy by removing restrictions on the private sector, reduce the role of the government in many areas and remove trade restrictions between India and other countries. India agreed to the conditionalities of World Bank and IMF and announced the New Economic Policy (NEP). The NEP consisted of wide ranging economic reforms. The thrust of the policies was towards creating a more competitive environment in the economy and removing the barriers to entry and growth of firms. This set of policies can broadly be classified into two groups: the stabilization measures and the structural reform measures. Stabilization measures are short-term measures, intended to correct some of the weaknesses that have developed in the balance of payments and to bring inflation under control. In simple words, this means that there was a need to maintain sufficient foreign exchange reserves and keep the rising prices under control. On the other hand, structural reform policies are long-term measures, aimed at improving the efficiency of the economy and increasing its international competitiveness by removing the rigidities in various segments of the Indian economy. The government initiated a variety of policies which fall under three heads, *viz.* liberalization, privatization and globalization.

Reforms in Various Sectors

Financial sector includes financial institutions, such as commercial banks, investment banks, stock exchange operations and foreign exchange market. The financial sector in India is regulated by the Reserve Bank of India (RBI). You may be aware that all banks and other financial institutions in India are regulated through various norms and regulations of the RBI. The RBI decides the amount of money that the banks can keep with themselves, fixes interest rates, nature of lending to various sectors etc. One of the major aims of financial sector reforms is to reduce the role of RBI from regulator to facilitator of financial sector. This means that the financial sector may be allowed to take decisions on many matters without consulting the RBI. The reform policies led to the establishment of private sector banks, Indian as well as foreign. Foreign investment limit in banks was raised to around 74 per cent. Those banks which fulfil certain conditions have been given freedom to set up new branches without the approval of the RBI and rationalize their existing branch networks. Though banks have been given permission to generate resources from India and abroad, certain managerial aspects have been retained with the RBI to safeguard the interests of the account-holders and the nation. Foreign Institutional Investors (FII), such as merchant bankers, mutual funds and pension funds, are now allowed to invest in Indian financial markets.

Reforms in Tax System

Tax reforms are concerned with the reforms in the government's taxation and public expenditure policies, which are collectively known as its fiscal policy. There are two types of taxes: direct and indirect. Direct taxes consist of taxes on incomes of individuals, as well as, profits of business enterprises. Since 1991, there has been a continuous reduction in the taxes on individual incomes as it was felt that high rates of income tax were an important reason for tax evasion. It is now widely accepted that moderate rates of income tax encourage savings and voluntary disclosure of income. The rate of corporation tax, which was very high earlier, has been gradually reduced. Efforts have also been made to reform the indirect taxes, taxes levied on commodities, in order to facilitate the establishment of a common national market for goods and commodities. In 2016, the Indian Parliament passed a law, *Goods and Services Tax Act, 2016*, to simplify and introduce a unified indirect tax system in India. This law came into effect from July 2017. This is expected to generate additional revenue for the government, reduce tax evasion and create 'one nation, one tax and one market'.

Another component of *reform* in this area is *simplification*. In order to encourage better compliance on the part of tax payers, many procedures have been simplified and the rates also substantially lowered.

Reforms in Foreign Exchange

The first important reform in the external sector was made in the foreign exchange market. In 1991, as an immediate measure to resolve the balance of payments crisis, the rupee was devalued against foreign currencies. This led to an increase in the inflow of foreign exchange. It also set the tone to free the determination of rupee value in the foreign exchange market from government control. Now, more often than not, markets determine exchange rates based on the demand and supply of foreign exchange.

Reform in Trade and Investment Policy

Liberalization of trade and investment regime was initiated to increase international competitiveness of industrial production and also foreign investments and technology into the economy. The aim was also to promote the efficiency of local industries and adoption of modern technologies. In order to protect domestic industries, India was following a regime of quantitative restrictions on imports. This was encouraged through tight control over imports and by keeping the tariffs very high. These policies reduced efficiency and competitiveness which led to slow growth of the manufacturing sector. The trade policy reforms aimed at: (i) dismantling of quantitative restrictions on imports and exports, (ii) reduction of tariff rates, and (iii) removal of licensing procedures for imports. Import licensing was abolished except in case of hazardous and environmentally sensitive industries. Quantitative restrictions on imports of manufactured consumer goods and agricultural products were also fully removed from April 2001. Export duties have been removed to increase the competitive position of Indian goods in the international markets.

Growth of GDP and Major Sectors

The reform process has completed three decades since its introduction. Let us now look at the performance of the Indian economy during this period. In economics, the growth of an economy is measured by the Gross Domestic Product. Look at Table 2.1. The post-1991 India witnessed a rapid growth in GDP on a continual basis for two decades. The growth of GDP increased from 5.6 per cent during 1980-1991 to 8.2 per cent during 2007-2012. During the reform period, the growth of agriculture has declined. While the industrial sector reported fluctuation, the growth of the service sector has gone up. This indicates that this growth is mainly driven by growth in the service sector. During 2012-2015, there has been a setback in the growth rates of different sectors witnessed post-1991. While agriculture recorded a high growth rate during 2013-14, this sector witnessed negative growth in the subsequent year. While the service sector continued to witness a high level of growth — higher than the overall GDP growth in 2014-15, this sector witnessed the high growth rate of 9.8 per cent. The industrial sector witnessed a steep decline during 2012-13, in the subsequent years it began to show a continuous positive growth.

Table 2.1: Growth of GDP and Major Sectors (in %)

Sector	*1980-91*	*1992-2001*	*2002-07*	*2007-12*	*2012-13*	*2013-14*	*2014-15*
Agriculture	3.6	3.3	2.3	3.2	1.5	4.2	–0.2*
Industry	7.1	6.5	9.4	7.4	3.6	5.0	7.0*
Services	6.7	8.2	7.8	10.0	8.1	7.8	9.8*
Total	**5.6**	**6.4**	**7.8**	**8.2**	**5.6**	**6.6**	**7.4**

Note. * Data pertaining to Gross Value Added (GVA). The GVA is estimated from GDP by adding subsidies on production and subtracting indirect taxes.

Source: Economic Survey for various years, Ministry of Finance, Government of India.

The opening of the economy has led to a rapid increase in foreign direct investment and foreign exchange reserves. The foreign investment, which includes foreign direct investment (FDI) and foreign institutional investment (FII), has increased from about US $100 million in 1990-91 to US $ 30 billion in 2017-18. There has been an increase in the foreign exchange reserves from about US $ 6 billion in 1990-91 to about US $ 413 billion in 2018-19. India is one of the largest foreign exchange reserve holders in the world. India is seen as a successful exporter of auto parts, engineering goods, IT software and textiles in the reform period. Rising prices have also been kept under control. On the other hand, the reform process has been widely criticized for not being able to address some of the basic problems facing our economy especially in areas of employment, agriculture, industry, infrastructure development and fiscal management.

Agriculture and Globalization

Reforms have not been able to benefit agriculture, where the growth rate has been decelerating. Public investment in agriculture sector especially in infrastructure, which includes irrigation, power, roads, market linkages and research and extension (which played a crucial role in the Green Revolution), has fallen in the reform period. Further, the partial removal of fertilizer subsidy has led to increase in the cost of production, which has severely affected the small and marginal farmers. This sector has been experiencing a number of policy changes such as reduction in import duties on agricultural products, low minimum support price and lifting of quantitative restrictions on the imports of agricultural products. These have adversely affected Indian farmers as they now have to face increased international competition. Moreover, because of export-oriented policy strategies in agriculture, there has been a shift from production for the domestic market towards production for the export market focusing on cash crops in lieu of production of food grains. This puts pressure on prices of food grains.

Globalization and Industry

Industrial growth has also recorded a slowdown. This is because of decreasing demand of industrial products due to various reasons such as cheaper imports, inadequate investment in infrastructure etc. In a globalized world, developing countries are compelled to open up their economies to greater flow of goods and capital from developed countries and rendering their industries vulnerable to imported goods. Cheaper imports have, thus, replaced the demand for domestic goods. Domestic manufacturers are facing competition from imports. The infrastructure, facilities, including power supply, have remained inadequate due to lack of investment. Globalization is, thus, often seen as creating conditions for the free movement of goods and services from foreign countries that adversely affect the local industries and employment opportunities in developing countries. Moreover, a developing country like India still does not have the access to developed countries' markets because of high non-tariff barriers. For example, although all quota restrictions on exports of textiles and clothing have been removed in India.

USA has not removed their quota restriction on import of textiles from India and China.

Effects of Globalization

Economic reforms have placed limits on the growth of public expenditure, especially in social sectors. The tax reductions in the reform period, aimed at yielding larger revenue and curb tax evasion, have not resulted in increase in tax revenue for the government. Also, the reform policies, involving tariff reduction, have curtailed the scope for raising revenue through custom duties. In order to attract foreign investment, tax incentives are provided to foreign investors which further reduced the scope for raising tax revenues. This has a negative impact on developmental and welfare expenditures.

The process of globalization through liberalization and privatization policies has produced positive, as well as, negative results both for India and other countries. Some scholars argue that globalization should be seen as an opportunity in terms of greater access to global markets, high technology and increased possibility of large industries of developing countries to become important players in the international arena. On the contrary, the critics argue that globalization is a strategy of the developed countries to expand their markets in other countries. According to them, it has compromised the welfare and identity of people belonging to poor countries. It has further been pointed out that market-driven globalization has widened the economic disparities among nations and people.

Viewed from the Indian context, some studies have stated that the crisis that erupted in the early 1990s was basically an outcome of the deep-rooted inequalities in Indian society and the economic reform policies initiated as a response to the crisis by the government, with externally advised policy package, further aggravated the inequalities. Further, it has increased the income and quality of consumption of only high-income groups and the growth has been concentrated only in some select areas in the services sector such as telecommunication, information technology, finance, entertainment, travel and hospitality services, real estate and trade, rather than vital sectors such as agriculture and industry which provide livelihoods to millions of people in the country.

Conclusion

Globalization is a complex process that is having a massive impact on living standards across both the developed and developing world. In general, the balance of evidence suggests that globalization is helping to reduce poverty and raise living standards. There is also, however, evidence that globalization has deleterious consequences as well. For example, in India, inter-regional inequality appears to have widened during the globalization era.

The challenge before India is in many ways unique. It is a country rich in knowledge and the production of technology. Historically, it has not, however, seen this knowledge as a commodity. In recent decades this has changed somewhat, and India has rapidly increased its integration with the global economy. Indeed the World Bank recently judged India to be one of the world's 'fast globalizers'. Despite the large steps taken by India recently, the rest of the world must recognize that India's democratic tradition, and its history of diverse views, means that the reforms will continue to be implemented unevenly, and slowly. India will, however, get there in the end.

REFERENCES

Books

Acharya, S. (2003). *India's Economy: Some Issues and Answers*, Academic Foundation, New Delhi.

Ahluwalia, I.J. and I.M.D. Little (1998). *India's Economic Reforms and Development*, Oxford University Press, New Delhi.

Alternative Survey Group (2005). *Alternative Economic Survey, India 2004-05*.

Bardhan, Pranab (1998). *The Political Economy of Development in India*, Oxford University Press, New Delhi.

Bhagwati, Jagdish (1992). *India in Transition: Freeing the Economy*, Oxford University Press, New Delhi.

Debroy, B. and Rahul Mukherji (Eds.) (2004). *The Political Economy of Reforms*, Book Well Publication, New Delhi.

Dreze, Jean and Amartya Sen (1996). *India: Economic Development and Social Opportunity*, Oxford University Press, New Delhi.

Dutt, Ruddar and K.P.M. Sundaram (2005). *Indian Economy*, S. Chand and Company, New Delhi.

Rao, C.H. Hanumantha and Hans Linnemann (1996). *Economic Reforms and Poverty Alleviation in India*, Sage Publication, Delhi.

Sachs, Jeffrey D., Ashutosh Varshney and Nirupam Bajpai (1999). *India in the Era of Economic Reforms*, Oxford University Press, New Delhi.

Government Reports and Websites

Appraisal Document of Twelfth Five Year Plan 2012-2017, NITI Aayog, Government of India, New Delhi. *https://dipam.gov.in*

Economic Survey for various years, Ministry of Finance, Government of India, Published by Oxford University Press, New Delhi.

Handbook of Statistics on Indian Economy, Reserve Bank of India for various years, Mumbai.

Tenth Five Year Plan 1997-2002, Planning Commission, Government of India, Vol. 1, New Delhi.

3

Impact of Economic Development in Home Appliances Market at India (Based on Business Forecasting Model)

Chinmoy Ghosh

Introduction

A company's strategy that trusts all of its marketing objectives into one inclusive strategy. There are many features that lead to the realization of a business in the industry. Marketing is one such important area that makes a business propagate. A good marketing plan should be stressed from bazaar investigation and emphasis on the correct product mix in order to reach the maximum profit prospective and survive the business. The marketing policy is the base of a marketing strategy.

In this chapter, we try to develop a concept of business trend analysis with the help of secondary data collected from DION report, CEAMA reports, P Morgan, Tech Naive, Spark Capital estimates etc. In that particular part of our research we used Ms-excel as well as statistical software tools to generate a business forecasting model of home appliances production trend to chalk out the development of business and economy of our country in near future.

Background and context of our study:

- The increasing electronics and consumer durables market in India presents a striking opportunity to manufacturers.
- Government of India's recently declared **Make in India** initiative has provided different stimulus to this sector.

Growing Industry

The demand for flat T.Vs, refrigerators, washing machines and air conditioners is on a rise with reduced penetration of products *vis-à-vis* global levels, rising disposable income and urbanization of consumers.

Market for white goods and televisions has been growing and high trend of probable production in the coming years.

Rising Imports to Meet Demand

There has been an upsurge in imports from low-cost regions such as China and South-East Asia due to various free trade agreements and readiness of products at a lower cost as associated to costs incurred in local manufacturing.

Production Growth to Bump into Local and Export Demand

To meet the rising home-grown demand and export demand to neighbouring regions and MEA, companies are planning to expand their local manufacturing in India and make the country an export hub.

Major Indian and global consumer durables companies have declared investments of around US 1.4 billion over the coming years in India.

The main three drivers to boost up Indian home appliance product market:

- *Sales replacement* techniques.
- *Market penetration* policy.
- *Low cost* mechanisms.

DRIVERS		
Large Component of Sales Comprises Secondary Sales Replacements — Significant Scope for Growing Primary Sales (First Time)	Market Penetration Lags Behind Global Average by up to 60% for Certain Categories	Primary Sales Driven by Low Cost Made for India and Made in India Products

Source: DION Report, EY Analysis.

Fig. 3.1: Drivers to Boost up Indian Home Appliance Products in Makret.

Objective of the Study

How the production of home appliance products will help our country (India) for economic development in near future.

Manufacturing Industry of Home Appliance Products in India at Present

How manufacturers face certain specific challenges:

1. Overturned duty structure due to FTAs makes Indian manufacturing uncompetitive for white goods such as washing machines, refrigerators and air conditioners.
2. Altered Modified Special Incentive Package Scheme (MSIPS) is currently not applicable to consumer durables such as washing machines, refrigerators and air conditioners.
3. Inadequate and underdeveloped local supplier base.
4. High cost of capital and other manufacturing costs due to frequently revised energy efficiency necessities.

India can emerge as the future manufacturing hub for the region, provided there is tolerable focus and support from the Government for this sector.

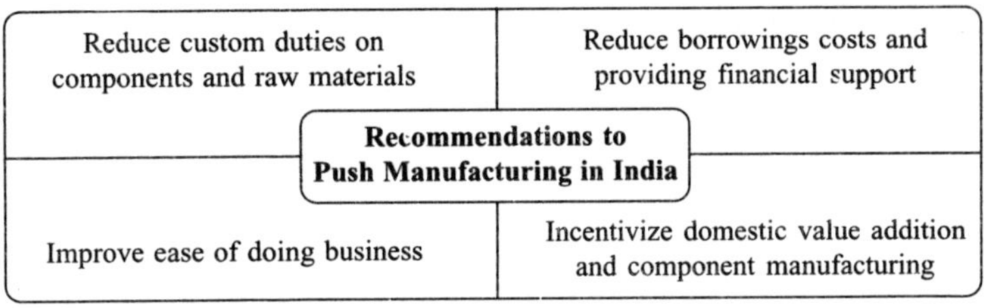

Fig. 3.2: Recommendations to Push Manufacturing Sector.

- The Indian consumer durables market has usually been a high employ, priority sector.
- Consumer durables account for more than 40 per cent of end consumer outlay in India.
- Annual turnover of more than INR 500 billion and contributes more than INR150 billion to revenue of Centre and State Governments.
- The sector pays more than 5.5 per cent of IIP.

It has been an employment originator — for every direct job.

Import concentrated sector and second top contributor to the current account deficit.

Urban markets justification for the majority share (65% of total revenues) in the consumer durables sector in India. . . .

. . . However, upcoming jet growth will come in from the rural markets (69% rural population).

Consumer Appliances
- Air conditioners
- Refrigerators
- Washing machines
- Sewing machines
- Electric fans
- Cleaning equipment
- Microwave ovens

Consumer Electronics
- TV
- Audio and video systems
- Electronic accessories
- CD and DVD playes
- Digital cameras
- Camcorders

Source: CEAMA reports, EY analysis.

Fig. 3.3: Jet Growth Sectors in Rural Market.

Business Trend of Home Appliances in India

The Indian consumer durables market has traditionally been a high employ, priority sector. Consumer durables account for more than 40 per cent of end consumer costs in India. Annual turnover of more than INR 500 billion and pays more than INR150 billion to revenue of Centre and State Governments, the sector pays more than 5.5 per cent of IIP. It has been an employment originator — for every direct job, 3 in-direct jobs are shaped. Import demanding sector and second top supplier Urban markets reason for the mainstream share (65% of total revenues) in the consumer durables segment in India . . . however, upcoming jet growth will originate subsequently in the rural markets (69% rural population).

Table 3.1: Revenue Generation from 2009 to 2016 for Selling of Home Appliances

Component	*2009*	*2013*	*2014*	*2015*	*2016*
Washing machine	37	87	101	122	140
Refrigerator	41	74	81	87	93
A.C.	68	77	86	96	108
T.V.	257	435	514	618	735

Source: JP Morgan, Tech Navio, Spark Capital Estimates, EY analysis.

In Fig. 3.4, there was a tremendous growth in turnover in respect of revenue generation from 2009 to 2016 for selling of home appliances washing machine, refrigerator, A.C. and T.V.

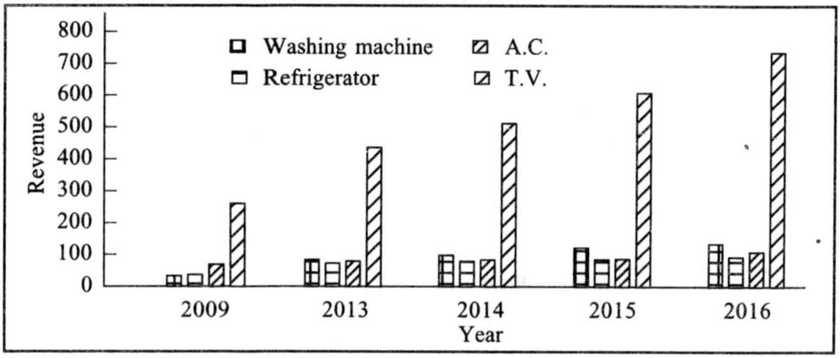

Fig. 3.4: Trend Analysis: Year-wise from 2009 to 2016.

Table 3.2: Market Penetration Analysis of Indian Home Appliances, in Respect of Global Market

Market Penetration	*India*	*Global Market*
Washing Machine	8.8	70
A.C.	3.0	60
Refrigerator	21.0	85
T.V.	60.0	89

Source: JP Morgan estimates, EY analysis.

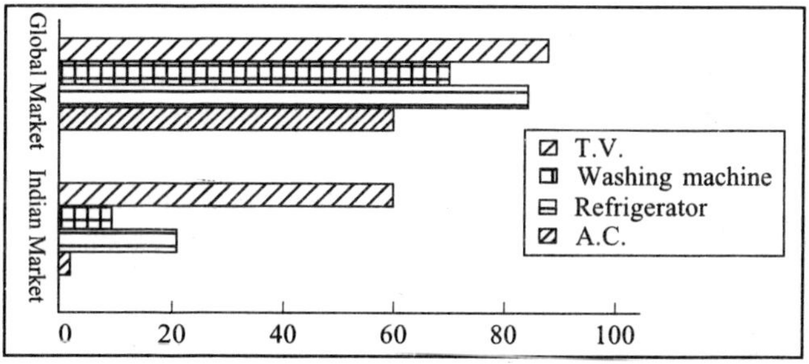

Fig. 3.5: Market Penetration: India *vs*. Global Market.

According to the comparison of market penetration global *versus* India, Fig. 3.5 shows that global market is more penetrated than that of Indian market but Indian market tries to roll on and penetrates according to the Indian and global markets.

The factors which relates the local demand and adoption of advanced technology home appliance products and their drivers:

Growth Drivers

Rise in Disposable Income — During 2013-2019, per capita income in India is probable to cultivate at a CAGR of approximately 6.6 per cent to around US $ 2,200 in 2019 from ~ US $ 1,500 in 2013. Growing trend of working women population will drive demand for home appliances such as washing machines.

Rise in Organized Retail — Planned retailing will not only modernize the supply chain, but also enable increased demand, specifically for high-end and branded products. Organized retail industry is probable to cover a market share of 15-18 per cent, from around 3 per cent currently by 2020.

Growing Demand — In rural markets, India's rural market accounting for approximately 69 per cent of India's households, chances for the consumer durables industry. Around 50 per cent of the rural population keeps a TV, 8 per cent owns refrigerators and around 1 per cent keeps washing machines. Moreover, increasing rural areas would increase the demand.

Urbanization and Greater Brand Awareness — The Indian urban population is predictable to increase from 31 per cent in 2011 to 41 per cent of the total population by 2030. Urban consumers have on-going to distinguish consumer durables as lifestyle products and are open to pay increased prices for branded products.

Product Modernization and Handiness of Newer Alternatives of Products — The consumer durables market is excess of products, each providing changed structures and technology, new choices and added benefits and has developed from a market with limited products and few features. The replacement cycle has condensed from 9-10 years to 4-5 years for most of the goods in this sector.

Narrowed Price Gap and Increased Affordability of Products Growth in Demand for Products — Once dignified luxuries, such as air-conditioners, washing machines and high end colour narrowed price gap. In the case of expensive consumer goods, retailers are providing to consumers by join forces with banks.

Table 3.3: Trend Analysis of Home Appliances Category-wise

Year	*A.C. Production*	*Washing Machine*	*Refrigerator*	*T.V.*
2010	1458	3049	8001	650
2011	2346	3080	8715	1170
2012	1666	2995	7738	1930
2013	1890	3225	8686	3090
2014	1948	3429	8421	4940

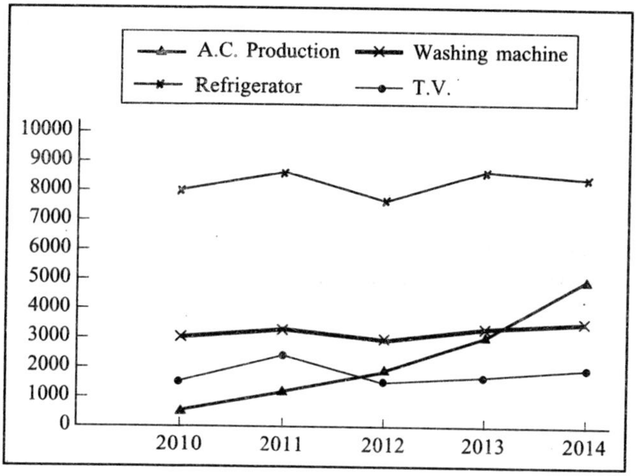

Fig. 3.6: Home Appliance Production.

Overall, growth in manufacturing over the 5 year period of FY10-FY14 has continued fairly reasonable, except for FPD TVs. Manufacturers put their plans on hold for growing capacity and investments that had been declared in 2008-10 period, due to demand slowdown given the weedy macroeconomic circumstances.

- Most manufacturers in India have been repeatedly their plants at ~ 80 per cent capacity, and trust on imports to meet local demand.
- There has been an important uptick in local manufacturing of T.Vs. due to reduction on custom duties on mechanisms and primarily last-mile gathering in the TV manufacturing industry.
- There is an important increase in localization in washing machine and refrigerator.

Analysis of Business Forecasting Model of Home Appliances in India

Business Forecasting Model of Air-conditioner Production 2015-2022

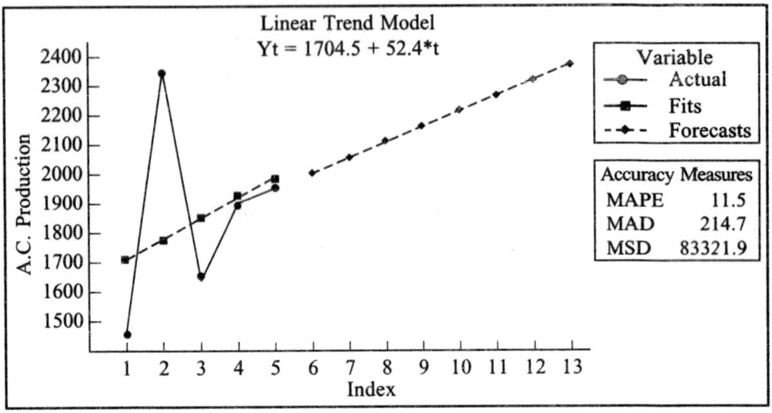

Fig. 3.7: Trend Analysis for Air-conditioner Production.

Data	A.C. PRODUCTION
Length	5
N Missing	0

Fitted Trend Equation: Yt = 1704.4 + 52.4*t

Accuracy Measures

MAPE	11.5
MAD	214.7
MSD	83321.9

Table 3.4: Forecasts of A.C. Production

Year	*Forecast of A.C. production*
2015	2018.8
2016	2071.2
2017	2123.6
2018	2176.0
2019	2228.4
2020	2280.8
2021	2333.2
2022	2385.6

The trend plot of Air-conditioner production that shows the original data, the fitted trend line, and forecasts. The Session window output also displays the fitted trend equation and three measures to help us determine the accuracy of the fitted values: MAPE, MAD, and MSD. The data of Air-conditioner production shows a general upward trend, though with an evident seasonal component. The trend model seems to fit fine to the whole trend.

Business Forecasting Model of Washing Machine Production from 2015-2022

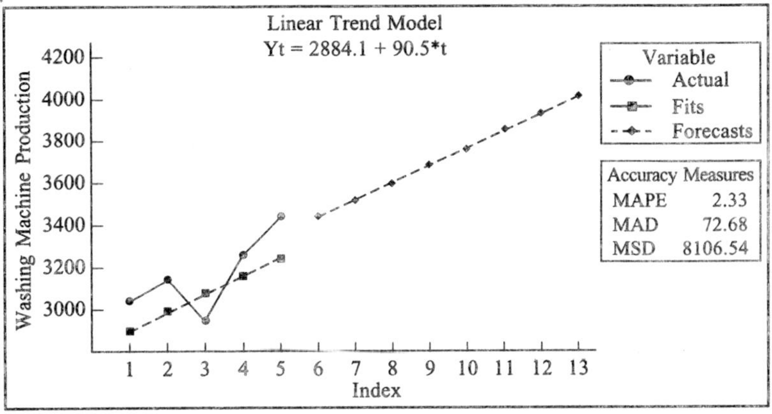

Fig. 3.8: Trend Analysis for Washing Machine Production.

Data	Washing Machine
Length	5
N Missing	0

Fitted Trend Equation: Yt = 2884.1 + 90.5*t

Accuracy Measures	
MAPE	2.33
MAD	72.68
MSD	8106.54

Table 3.5: Forecasts of Washing Machine Production during 2015-2022

Year	*Forecast of washing machine production*
2015	3427.1
2016	3517.6
2017	3608.1
2018	3698.6
2019	3789.1
2020	3879.6
2021	3970.1
2022	4060.6

The Washing Machine data shows a general upward trend, though with an evident seasonal component. The trend model seems to fit fine to the total trend. The Session window output also displays the fitted trend equation and three measures to help us determine the accuracy of the fitted values based on MAPE, MAD, and MSD.

Business Forecasting Model of Refrigerator Production from 2015-2022

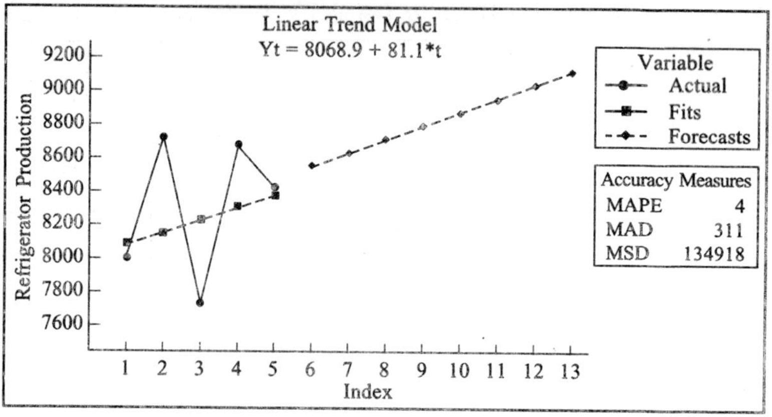

Fig. 3.9: Trend Analysis for Refrigerator Production.

Data	Refrigerator
Length	5
N Missing	0

Fitted Trend Equation: Yt = 8068.9 + 81.1*t

Accuracy Measures	
MAPE	4
MAD	311
MSD	134918

Table 3.6: Forecast of Refrigerator Production during 2015-2022

Year	*Forecast of refrigerator production*
2015	8555.5
2016	8636.6
2017	8717.7
2018	8798.8
2019	8879.9
2020	8961.0
2021	9042.1
2022	9123.2

Interpreting the Results

The refrigerator production data shows a general upward trend, though with an evident seasonal component. The trend model seems to fit fine to the total trend. The Session window output also displays the fitted trend equation and three measures to help us determine the accuracy of the fitted values based on MAPE, MAD, and MSD.

Business Forecasting Model of Television Production from 2015-2022

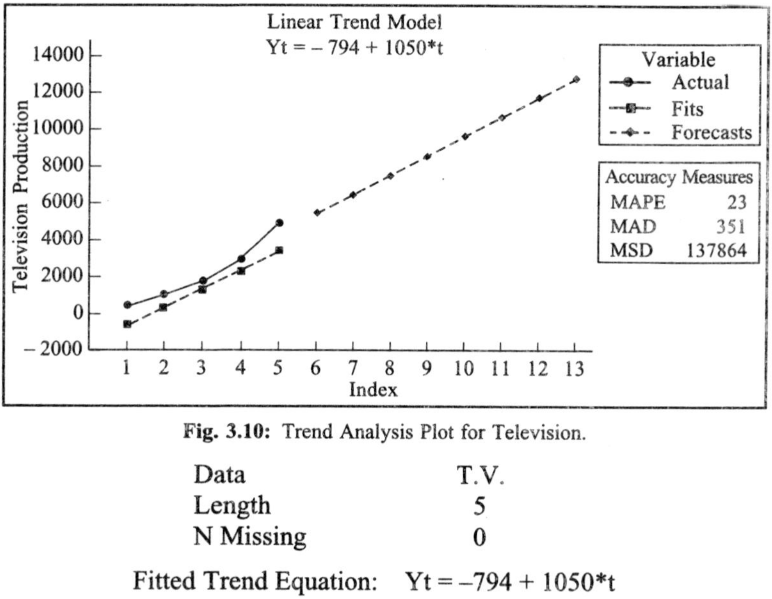

Fig. 3.10: Trend Analysis Plot for Television.

Data	T.V.
Length	5
N Missing	0

Fitted Trend Equation: Yt = –794 + 1050*t

Accuracy Measures	
MAPE	23
MAD	351
MSD	137864

Table 3.7: Forecasts of T.V. Production during 2015-2022

Year	*Forecast of T.V. production*
2015	5506
2016	6556
2017	7606
2018	8656
2019	9706
2020	10756
2021	11806
2022	12856

The Television set production data shows a general upward trend, though with an evident seasonal component. The trend model seems to fit fine to the total trend. The Session window output also displays the fitted trend equation and three measures to help us determine the accuracy of the fitted values based on MAPE, MAD, and MSD.

Conclusion

The trend model provides us a path how production of home appliance products will boost up the production trend and which will lead to economic development in our country in near future. The Indian consumer durables market has traditionally been a high employ, priority sector. Consumer durables account for more than 40 per cent of end consumer costs in India. Annual turnover of more than INR 500 billion and pays more than INR 150 billion to revenue of Centre and State governments, the sector pays to more than 5.5 per cent of IIP. It has been an employment originator — for every direct job, 3 in-direct jobs are shaped. Import demanding sector and second top supplier Urban markets reason for the mainstream share (65% of total revenues) in the consumer durables segment in India. However, upcoming jet growth will originate subsequently in the rural markets (69% rural population).

REFERENCES

Anthony, O. Putman, *Marketing Your Services: A Step-by-step Guide for Small Businesses and Professionals*, New York: Wiley, c1990. *MBS 658.8 PUTN*

Catherine DeVrye, *Goods Service is Good Business: 7 Simple Strategies for Success*, 2nd ed., Frenchs Forest, N.S.W.: Prentice Hall, 2000. *MBS Mt Eliza 658.812 DEVR [2000]*

Hellen Woodruffe, *Service Marketing*, Macmillan India Ltd., Delhi, 1997.

Jeffrey, F. Rayport and Bernard, J. Jaworski, *Best Face Forward: Why Companies must Improve their Service Interfaces with Customers*, Boston, MA: Harvard Business School Press, c2005. *MBS 658.812 RAYP [2005]*

Jha, S.M., *Service Marketing*, Himalaya Publishing House, Mumbai, 2000.

M. John and A. Czepiel, *Cambridge, Managing Customer Satisfaction in Consumer Service Business*, Mass.: Marketing Science Institute, 1980. *MBS f 658.812 CZEP*

Malcolm, H.B., McDonald with John W. Leppar, *How to Sell a Service: Guidelines for Effective Selling in a Service Business*, 2nd ed., Oxford: Heinemann Professional, 1988. *MBS 658.85 MCDO*

Mark Gabbott and Gillian Hogg, *Consumers and Services*, Chichester; New York: J. Wiley, c1998. *MBS 658.812 GABB*

Payne Adrian, *The Essence of Service Marketing*, Prentice-Hall of India, New Delhi.

4

Financial Literacy in the Light of Adapting to Globalization and the Cyber World Threats

Meaning and Concept

Shawkat Ali

Introduction

The process through which people, ideas and goods spread throughout the world is called Globalization. It promotes more integration and interaction between the world's cultures, governments and economies, which leads to the adoption of open and free trading markets. Which minimizes trade barriers, removes capital controls, and liberalized foreign exchange restrictions. Globalization transform the habits, necessities, opportunities and behaviour of persons and the organization and the different kinds of cyber world threats involved to it. Cyber world threats actually means different kinds of risk involved regarding financial loss, decline to the reputation of any organization from any kind of failure of its information technology systems. Proper implementation and monitoring of appropriate system of financial literacy stimulates different factors of an active citizenship like socially accountable behaviour, decision, support, better mobility and the increase of moral principles, which leads to the improvement of understanding of financial products and concepts of persons and the organization and ultimately lowers the risk involved in the field regarding financial activity. The financial literacy is accredited worldwide as an significant element of the monetary and economic firmness and progress. It can't be denied that financially literate individuals and organizations contribute positively to an effective function of the financial system.

Review of the Literature

Ramadevi, V. and Selvaraj, S.N. (2011) have provided a work on "Impact of Globalization on Financial Service Sector". They have argued that with the emergence of various financial institutions and regulatory bodies, financial services sectors become very dynamic, which ultimately leads towards economic liberalization. For this reason innovation is must. They have depicted service sector contribute 8.8 per cent of GDP. In the new environment of globalization financial service providers has emphasized on technologically advanced and feature-rich solutions. They have tried to examine the status of financial service industry in India and to study the challenges before them due to globalization.

Starcek Simon and Trunk Ales (2013) have provided a work on "The Meaning and Concept of Financial Education in the Society of Economic Changes". They have opined that globalization has modified the habits, requirements, expectations and behaviour of individuals and the risk involved to it. They have argued that different factor of an active citizenship can be stimulated by financial education and it also lowers the risk involved to it significantly. They have told that financial literacy is acknowledged worldwide as an important element of the economic and financial stability and development. They have opined that financial education is lifelong process. They have tried to present the meaning of financial education and advantage of it in the arena of economic changes for individuals, economy and society.

Objective of the Study

The chapter presents the meaning and concept of financial literacy and the advantages of financial literacy for individuals, organizations, nation and society in the light of adapting to globalization and the cyber world threats.

Methodology of the Study

This chapter does not intend to build a new theory and it is based on available secondary data and secondary data source include books, articles, research papers and internet.

Elaborative Discussion

Financial literacy enhances the ability of understanding how money works, how someone makes, manages and invests money, and also expends it to help others. Financial literacy refers to the ability to understand and apply different financial skills effectively, including personal financial management, budgeting, and saving. Financial literacy implies the ability of understanding and use various financial skills effectively, including personal financial management, budgeting, and investing. Financial literacy is crucial as it equips you with the knowledge and tools needed to make strong informed decisions. Without it, the financial decisions we do make, or do not make, can potentially threaten your financial security. According to the Financial Literacy and Education Commission, there are five key components of financial literacy, namely earn, spend, save and invest, borrow, and protect. Financial literacy equips us with the knowledge and skills that so needed to manage money effectively. Without it, our financial decisions and the actions we take — or do not take — lack a solid foundation for success. Financial literacy is the ability to know how to manage your financial resources. Financial education is the ability to understand how financial resources work. It refers to the technique of investing and managing financial resources and the skill to make good financial decisions. Financial literacy can be an equalizer for individuals. Financial literacy empowers us with the knowledge that we can be smart with our finances. It makes us mindful about debt, encourages us to save early and often, and helps us form a plan and track to our personal financial goals. There are abundant studies that illustrate the very real impact of financial literacy: improved rates of savings, lower levels of debt, increased rates of asset accumulation, just to name a few. It affects your ability to provide for yourself and family, your attitude to money and investment, as well as your contribution to your community. Financial literacy enhances the ability of the people to understand what is needed to them to achieve a lifestyle which is financially balanced, sustainable, ethical and responsible. There are six foundational principles that can be used to study finance: money has a time value; the higher the reward, the greater the risk; diversification of investments can reduce overall risk; financial markets are efficient in pricing securities; a manager's and stockholders' objectives may differ; and reputation . Gilbert moonlighted as a personal finance author, and in 1849, he published an article titled "Ten Minutes' Advice about Keeping a Banker". In it, he detailed the advantages of having a bank account and narrated the technique for those who might be intimidated.

A good financial plan contains seven key components:

1. Budgeting and taxes.
2. Managing liquidity, or ready access to cash.
3. Financing large purchases.
4. Managing your risk.
5. Investing your money.
6. Planning for retirement and the transfer of your wealth.
7. Communication and record keeping.

The need for financial literacy is witnessed by the poor financial condition of individuals: burden of debt without a budget plan and making wrong decisions about their money capital. Most of these poor financial behaviours originates due to financial illiteracy. It includes understanding of how a running bank account works, using a credit card really means, and how to get rid of such debt. In sum, financial literacy has an impact on families as they try to balance their budget, buy a home, fund their children's education, and ensure an income at retirement.

Ten essential tips to teach our children to save money:

1. Discuss Wants *versus* Needs.
2. Let them Earn their Own Money.
3. Set Savings Goals.
4. Provide a Place to Save.
5. Have them Track Spending.
6. Offer Savings Incentives.
7. Leave Room for Mistakes.
8. Act as their Creditor.
9. Talk about Money.
10. Set a Good Example.

Some ways to teach our young children financial responsibility are to show them the value of savings. It is only natural for money to burn a hole in the pockets of the youngest kids, let them earn a little extra, you probably expect your kids to clean their room, help with the dishes and do other daily chores, introduce philanthropy, create learning opportunities. It helps us understand the value of money. When we understand the value of money, we are able to handle our finances in a better way. This is because they understand the value of money and how difficult it is to earn it. To sum it up, youth financial literacy in 2021 is very important. Ages 3 to 4: Introduce the Concept of Money and

Exchanging It for Goods. The best time to start teaching your kids about money is the age they begin to count, says Joy Liu, a trainer at a financial planning company called the Financial Gym. Start by having them count and sort coins.

Financial literacy is important because it equips one with the knowledge and skill to manage money effectively. Without financial literacy, the actions and decisions one make or do not make with respect to savings and investments would lack a strong foundation. Financially, literate consumers can manage money with confidence, which means effectively allocating their earnings to their goals and limiting or attacking their debt. Here are the ways financial literacy can affect your life:

1. *Understand how to budget:* To pay for expenses, save or get rid of debt, you must understand how much income you are taking in and distribute it effectively. Making a budget is your first step towards a true understanding of money management. Once you have a budget, you can continue to track spending and revisit your spending plan regularly. There are many budgeting methods (zero-based, two-account etc.), so choose the one that you are most likely to stick to.
2. *Understand and manage debt:* When you are financially literate, you recognize the importance of seeking out the lowest interest rates when comparing loan terms. You also know that paying off credit card balances each month is your best bet for preventing interest charges and high credit utilization, which affects your credit score. If you already have debt, financial literacy can help you choose the best methods to get out of debt, either on your own or with the help of financial products such as debt consolidation loans or balance transfer credit cards.
3. *Understand how an emergency fund works:* A crucial way to prevent debt from building is to create an emergency fund, a savings account that you can draw from when unexpected expenses arise. A financially literate saver knows how much to set aside— ideally three to six months' worth of expenses — and replenishes it when necessary.
4. *Plan for retirement:* While developing an emergency savings account, saving for retirement should be a concurrent long-term goal. When you have become financially literate, you can calculate how much to save and which types of accounts will help you get there.

Financial Literacy has become one of the top priorities for most of the countries today as it is directly proportional to the economic growth of a country. It is alarming to know that the financial literacy rate in India is way behind other countries. According to a global survey, India is home to almost 20 per cent of the world's population, however, 76 per cent of its adult population is not even aware of the basic financial concepts. The survey reports that Financial Literacy in India has been signification poor compared to the rest of the world. Financial Literacy is the ability to understand basic financial concepts and the possession of knowledge and skills required to make informed and effective financial planning, decisions using the available financial resources. It is about knowjng how to generate, spend, invest and save money. It is the ability to manage your finances well by making the optimum use of the available financial products and resources to give you maximum benefit. In India, Financial Literacy has still not become a priority like other developed nations. Lack of basic financial knowledge results in poor investments and financial decisions. That is why most of the people invest in short-term plans and physical assets to accomplish their personal goals which give lesser benefits and does not help in the economic development of the country. According to a global survey, about a staggering 76 per cent of Indian adults do not understand basic financial concepts and are unfortunately financially illiterate even today. The survey confirms the financial literacy rate in India has been consistently poor as compared to the rest of the world. It is indeed high time for a developing country like India to realize the importance of financial literacy as such poor financial literacy rate can prove to be a major setback to India's ambition of becoming an economic superpower in the coming years. Financial Literacy has become one of the topmost priorities for most nations today as understanding basic financial concepts allows people to manage their wealth in a more organized way which in turn helps in the economic growth of the nation. It is proved that people with appropriate financial education and knowledge make better financial planning and makes the most of the available financial resources for maximum benefit. In the United States of America, financial literacy was initiated way back in 1908 by the American Credit Union Movement. In 1957, financial education was made mandatory by the state of Nevada and then other states followed. Australia also provides financial literacy education through customized programmes. Singapore and Indonesia are among few of the Asian countries who have started this initiative and have taken the first step towards Financial Literacy. Cybercrime cost the global economy as much as $600 billion in 2017. New technologies and connections mean new threats to some countries and new opportunities to others. Cybercrime impacts nearly every location on the globe. Cybercrime has a direct and significant impact on jobs, innovation, economic growth, and investment. Additionally, IP theft makes up at least 25 per cent of cybercrime costs, and has an especially high threat to military technology. Two areas of cybercrime that are difficult to measure are IP theft and loss of opportunity. Cyber attacks may have some motivation behind them as they may be processed unknowingly. The attacks that are processed knowingly can be considered as cyber crime and they have serious impacts on the society in the form of economical disrupt, psychological disorder, threat to National security etc. Major causes of cyber crimes are cyber criminals are always on a lookout for ways to make huge money through easy approaches such as easy access system, storing data in a small space, complex codings, negligence, loss of evidence, evolution of cyber crime. For decades, governments have increased their cyber security budgets for national defence, but not invested enough to teach citizens adequate cyber-skills despite our growing reliance on the internet. This stance has contributed to cyber attacks becoming one of the fastest growing crimes, costing an estimated $600 billion globally in 2017. The situation has become even more pressing during the pandemic as our reliance on the internet has grown. Millions of people globally now depend on it for work, school, health, and basic services. Yet many do not understand the risks and lack the skills to keep themselves, their communities and their employers safe. Governments need to improve cyber security by using the same strategies introduced to make driving safer. Just as governments mandate airbags and sensors in cars, they should require building more secure digital devices. Just as drivers and passengers are taught how to wear seat belts and to follow the rules of the road, citizens should be taught how to safely navigate the internet highway. A small group of nations are moving in the right direction and can show others how best to proceed, according to our Cyber Risk Literacy and Education Index, which ranks 50 geographies, including the European Union. Switzerland, Singapore, the United Kingdom, Australia and the Netherlands topped the list because of their strong government policies, education systems, widespread access to training and citizen support to reduce risk.

To date, most governments' strategies to improve cyber security overlook the importance of continued cyber-risk education for its citizens across all ages and social demographics. Many countries publish policies and motivational plans, but few include actual steps or consistent funding to complete the work. Only eight countries in our index had publicly available metrics to measure their progress regarding cyber-risk literacy and education goals. Yet studies show that 95 per cent of cyber security issues can be traced to human error. Teaching basic skills such as using strong passwords, identifying phishing scams and understanding how data is gathered and how a digital identity is tracked online can dramatically improve the cyber security and the safety of a nation's citizens. Switzerland, which ranked first in the index, has made specific goals and transparency a priority. It has a comprehensive 80-page implementation document that lays out departmental responsibilities, and what national or provincial legislation is required. Specific milestones are set, and a timeline assigned to ensure accountability. The education efforts appear to be working: Data from Kaspersky and Microsoft showed that that Swiss citizens were among the least likely to fall a foul of malware or infection. The more successful nations create an office that is responsible for ensuring that citizens receive the cyber-risk education they need, whether they are kindergarteners or retirees. Singapore, ranked second in the index, established the Cyber Security Agency of Singapore to keep its cyberspace safe and secure. The nation is educating citizens in large part because internet use is high, and its global financial centre is at risk of attack. Its cyber-wellness courses occur over multiple grades, and focus on social and practical safety tips such as understanding cyber-bullying. Too often governments focus on the cost of cyber-risk education rather than on the positive impact it could have on the economy. Yet eighth-ranked Israel shows how a well-educated population and connected institutions can contribute significantly to the national economy by providing more jobs and greater innovation. The country prioritizes cyber security education earlier than most countries and assesses the cyber-risk literacy of children and youth at key points in their development and education. This investment in human resources has led to a wealth of cyber-related innovation and economic growth. As we utilize more sophisticated digital and data-rich technologies, we need to protect our institutions, our communities, and ourselves from cybercrime. Companies should build more secure devices, infrastructure and data-processing capabilities. In turn, governments need to do their part by ensuring that all citizens get the education they need to remain safe online.

Globalization and Financial Stability

One specific mechanism through which globalization can affect economic growth, poverty and inequality is its impact on financial stability.

Financial crises can result in a permanent loss of income, have a devastating effect on poverty and increase inequality. Financial globalization is an aggregate concept that refers to increasing global linkages created through cross-border financial flows. Financial integration refers to an individual country's linkages to international capital markets. Along with good employment prospects, financial education can play a key role in helping individuals and families build their assets. Moreover, well-informed financial consumers ultimately lead to better financial markets, where rogue products are forced from the market-place and confidence is raised. Globalization helps developing countries to deal with rest of the world increase their economic growth, solving the poverty problems in their country. The developed countries were able to invest in the developing nations, creating job opportunities for the poor people. Globalization is a combination of gross domestic product (GDP), industrialization, and the Human Development Index (HDI). Developed nations benefit under globalization•as businesses compete worldwide, and from the ensuing reorganization in production, international trade, and the integration of financial markets. Globalization allows a multinational corporation to make a product in one country and sell it in another. This provides jobs in one country and less expensive goods in the other. Globalization also allows for the free flow of capital between countries, which many believe spurs economic growth. Benefits of globalization are access to new cultures, the spread of technology and innovation, lower costs for products, higher standards of living across the globe, access to new markets, access to new talent, international recruiting, managing employee immigration. Along with good employment prospects, financial education can play a key role in helping individuals and families build their assets. Moreover, well informed financial consumers ultimately lead to better financial markets, where rogue products are forced from the market-place and confidence is raised.

Suggestions

A higher level of financial literacy has an effect on the individual's improving of understanding financial products, notions and risks. On the basis of received information, instructions and objective advice the skills and confidence for strengthening the awareness about financial risks and opportunities can be developed more effective. Financial literate individuals are better acquainted where to find help and they can take more effective measures to improve their wealth.

Some important ways to improve your financial literacy:

1. Subscribe to financial newsletters. For free financial news in your inbox, try subscribing to financial newsletters from trusted sources.
2. Listen to financial podcasts.
3. Read personal finance books.
4. Use social media.
5. Start keeping a budget.
6. Talk to a financial professional.

Anti-virus software is designed to prevent malicious software programmes from embedding on your computer. If it detects malicious code, like a virus or a worm, it works to disarm or remove it. Anti-virus software is the next line of defence so that cyber criminals who exploit flaws in software packages may be thwarted. In parallel, banks need to conduct awareness programmes for their customers and encourage them to report phishing mails/phishing sites, highlight the risks of sharing their online account credentials, passwords, and other measures they can take to protect themselves from fraudsters and people with *mala fide* intent. Five ways to protect your business from cybercrime:

1. Keep all softwares updated and regularly patched.
2. Invest in a reliable VPN.
3. Educate and train your staff.
4. Divide, encrypt, and back up sensitive data.
5. Set-up strict limitations on company computers.

REFERENCES

Ramadevi, V. and Selvaraj, S.N., "Impact of Globalization on Financial Service Sector", February 2011, *Conference. Global Business Environment and Its Impact on Management Education*, At Periyar University, Salem, Volume 1.

Starcek Simon and Trunk Ales, "The Meaning and Concept of Financial Education in the Society of Economic Changes", June 2013, *Conference: Active Citizenship by Knowledge Management & Innovation: Proceedings of the Management, Knowledge and Learning International Conference 2013 (Make Learn)*, At: Zadar, Croatia.

https://theprint.in/india/why-cyber-risk-education-is-the-new-form-of-literacy-countries-must-keep-up-with/577784/

https://www.experian.com/blogs/ask-experian/what-is-financial-literacy-and-why-is-it-important/

https://www.google.com/search?sxsrf

https://yourstory.com/mystory/why-is-financial-literacy-important-in-india-58xfag1ewi

www.epw.org.in

www.rbi.org.in

Section – II

Social and Cultural Aspects of Globalization

5

Impact of Globalization in day-do-day Life

Kanchana Dodan Godage

I will be talking about the globalization and its impacts on our day-to-day life with my own observations and experiences. Before going to recall my own observations on globalization, I would like to see how it has been defined. There are many ways that are used to define the concept of globalization in the social science literature. I would like to quote the prominent sociologist, Anthony Giddens' definition on globalization. For Giddens, globalization means "the intensification of worldwide social relations which link distant localities in such a way that local happenings are shaped by events occurring many miles away and *vice versa*" (Steger, 2009:13).

In other words, I would say it is a process which tries to intensify the societal relationship from different aspects such as economic, political, cultural, ecological etc. What would be then the means for such intensification? If it is a process or a system, it should have means to operate. To me, those means can be the technology and the techniques.

My next question is that who is then operating this process or the system? Who are the actors? We should identify from where these global changes come to us by forcing to be changed. Who did the changes first? Is it a myth or a god given thing? Prior to the answers of these questions let's move our attention on how the famous political scientist, Harold D. Lasswell has defined the term politics in 1936 in his book called *Politics: Who Gets What, When, How*. Later, the title of the book has become as his definition on politics. He said. politics means that elites' behaviour and their activities which are based on the political power of the society. For him, each activity of the political system will be depending on political power. Elites have access for that, and they use that power to influence the decision making and implementation process of a country so that politics means the struggle for political power or the activities which are surrounded by elites in the society. In the same way, I would say, globalization means that who gets what, when and how. The powerful elites in the international arena either influence the decisions of the international world or they themselves create decisions.

So, international elites consist of not only the powerful states like United States of America, United Kingdom etc. but also it can be like multinational and transnational companies.

When and how sooner the changes happen in the international arena (due to so-called intensification), we as the periphery level countries in the world would receive them through the means of globalization. How sooner the changes are going to be happened within us we use to call it modernization. Those changes may be visible among us through different means of communication, dressings, attitudes, music, degrees, disciplines etc. This two-day international seminar and the participation of myself have also happened as an impact of the globalization.

We may have immensely tasted the outputs and outcomes of this global process in our day-to-day life. Hereinafter, I will be focusing on few of my observations on impacts of globalization during my day-to-day life.

It has been immensely grown the fast-food culture in Sri Lanka against the traditional world-famous Sri Lankan Spicy food which is mostly helping to maintain the health of the human body. So, non-communicable diseases have increased day-by-day in the Sri Lankan society. As explained by the prominent American sociologist George Ritzer, McDonaldization — expansion of the fast-food-restaurants has been a serious issue to convert or change the healthy food habits into the *KFC, Hamburger, Chips/Fries* etc.

I used to observe the obesity of my neighbour-house-son daily. He usually orders more than four *Pizzas* per month using his mother's credit card. When his mother realizes that there is no time to cancel the orders since as soon as the online booking is done the *Pizza* is at home within 5 to 10 minutes. You might have also seen the *Pizza*-men who usually move here and there delivering *Pizzas* by motorbikes wearing the *pizza*-bag which says that *Eat me within 5 minutes* . . . like. This grade-six-old boy, maybe, he never expected to be, or he is not thinking about his appearance at all, is greedy with *Pizzas*. The family seems to be broken so that the father is not living with them and his mother seems busy with her smart phone all the time. The boy is addicted, and whatever greedy things are done through her credit card. Thus, we cannot only see the wrong side of the globalization. In this case, easy access, Online shopping, use of Credit cards can also be considered as the positive aspects of globalization.

My second observation found when I was teaching at the undergraduate classes. While, teaching my students when I was moving through the lectures from slide to slide. Even though I said very clearly at the beginning of the class that I am going to give all slides to them, they tried to capture each slide using their smart phones. When they were making their hands up at once and snapping my slides in the classroom, I felt like that the paparazzi are in the classroom following my slides. When I checked with them whether they can recall what they have captured, it was very sad, and that practice has just been style. However, it was bit uncomfortable to me in the very first day, but, now-a-days, I can bear it. Also, use of e-learn platforms, digital library, portable dictionaries and most of the learning facilities are in-built with their smart phones, but still usage of them can be very less and consume most of their learning hours with social media like *Facebook, WhatsApp, Messenger* etc. Even though the formal and informal educational methods have been increasingly enhanced by technology, however, due to more popularity of social media less attention for the formal educational methods can be seen. In the Open and Distance Learning context, what I found was that the cost and the time which were used to create and maintain the learn platforms are not benefited by the learners to the level of satisfaction in achieving the expected outcomes.

When it comes to the plagiarism, they are also capable of reproducing the knowledge of others. Once I thought, to avoid plagiarism and allowing them to be more critical on their writing, I directed them to go to the field to meet the grassroots level administrative officer (We call him *Grama Niladhari* in Sinhala) who is as the village headman for few villages. I asked my students to conduct an interview and find out the administrative difficulties which are faced by him. So, each student had to meet the *Grama Niladhari* — so-called village headman in his or her area. They also had to report me on how they conducted the interviews and what were the methodologies adopted. You don't believe that more than 10 per cent of the students found that they have prepared the essays, but by digging the internet to find out similar kind of someone else's interviews and even without acknowledging them. Nonetheless, the Google or whatever search engines which helped them to prepare their assignments by being home, were also helping me to find out them as wrong doers. I know that this is not only common to Sri Lanka but also to everywhere in the world.

Once, when I was asking from one of my teachers when he was in a tremendous thinking, why and what was the matter? He replied me saying that I am thinking of my daughter's hot-tea-image which was sent to me to hint that she is enjoying her tea-time at her university cafeteria in Melbourne. But my mind is not yet satisfied with that. My emotion or my utmost eager by being here is to hear her voice. See how the technology creates the emotional gap in the relationships. Not only that, when Western mothers are comfortable with staying at adult care houses in their adult age, when kids of Asian parents with Westernized mind-set, when they think that their parents are also no longer need to be stayed all the time with them and can be even in adult care homes, parents get anxious and disappointed. Of course, we cannot blame on our parents, maybe adult-care-home culture of us are very worst when it compares with the Westernized adult-care-home culture. So, ladies and gentlemen, you might also be proud, and you will also in future encourage your kids to have not only local education but also to go abroad and complete the education. But remember that they would not just learn and come, they will be coming back with the Western cultural practices. Their dressing, thinking, sensitivity etc. will be so different with the Asian practices. These are very visible changes and outcomes of globalization.

The process of globalization has also intensified the changes in administrative behaviour; it has doubled the work with huge repetition. Since 1950, when the global pressures came to change, slim or reduce the size of the public sector of many of the countries like us, due to the contextual mismatch, as commented by Willy McCourt interestingly in his article "*Finding a way forward on public employment reform: A Sri Lankan case study*", "all reform efforts have come in a series of waves. . . . Unfortunately, like waves in the ocean they receded as fast as they came" (McCourt: N.D., 7). However, even though there is not a consistency, the introduction of the Information and Communication Technology can be seen here and there in the public sector services. Due to majority's distrust towards believing the technology they do the same work manually as well. People mostly as service seekers used to ignore the e-services.

So, What Went Wrong?

According to the renowned political ecologist, Fred W. Riggs, developing societies like us have named as prismatic. When light send through a prism, fused, prismatic and diffracted stages can be seen. Fused societies are equal to underdeveloped countries and the developed societies are included to the diffracted category. We, prismatic societies are in the transformative stage of the development. We have both qualities of the developed and underdeveloped societies. To me, it is true, and we have become like victims of the globalization. We have either lost or purely ignored the indigenous economic sources. What we have experienced as the modernization is not deeply rooted. The changes in which we experience are only happened onto the surface. Unless we address the social issues such as social poverty, discrimination, discrepancies in the resource allocation, unemployment etc. through the structural changes, nation building will not be a real. We still have the structures which were adopted by the colonial rulers. Cultural plurality seems to be the national identity for many of the Third World countries. It was the practice and the belief that had from the ancient period. Colonial rulers who came to our societies identified us as the uncivilized communities since our skin colour, behaviour, belief, culture etc. were not much same as of them. When they began to civilize us, our inherited cultural dignity also began to be broken. We have lost the most significant thing — social coherence. That has not been happened as a sudden, but it took a long period to be worst. Now the most interesting thing is that the same global forces through new means asking us to be united for social harmony.

Let me once to share my own experience with you. Very recently, one of my fellow academics was claiming on her students that she could not teach racism at the class since the Sinhalese as most of the class got hurt and started provoking her. My answer was that if we as teachers, academics, consultants, scholars, educators etc. cannot teach racism without hurting the minority or majority, we, as teachers, are failed in teaching. I also hate the educational institutes which propagate ethnic or religious based education by targeting one religion or one ethnic group. This practice was, however, begun with extremism from the colonial period. Education should be opened for all ethnic groups — especially, from primary level to tertiary level education. Then only we can learn from each other. We will feel pain, happiness, sadness of other ethnic groups. We will not suspect each other. We will not feel any kind of extreme behaviour towards others. Marriages, food habits, dressing, festivals etc. and narrow mindset will be changed. If we understand the beauty of that togetherness, then, a country's nation building would be easier. Regional cooperation would be easier, and we can talk about the global citizenship as well.

Finally, globalization is a process of changing the world behaviour. We should bear those changes willingly or unwillingly. It was people or countries in the world periphery can have at least a balance approach in adopting the global changes while protecting the national identities that would greatly help to not to have sudden shocks in the national culture, economy or politics.

REFERENCES

McCourt, Willy (N.D.), *Finding a Way Forward on Public Employment Reform: A Sri Lankan Case Study*, University of Manchester: Institute for Development Policy and Management.

Steger, Manfred B. (2009), *Globalization: A Very Short Introduction*, New York: Oxford University Press.

6

Globalization, Cultural Pluralism and National Identity

Socio-Economic and Historical Perspectives

Kallol Bandyopadhyay

The Flowing River of Bengali Culture and the Ocean of Globalization — A Tale

In the institutionalized academic world in India, the conventional tale of advent of globalization and expansion of its empire started with Manmohan Singh's economic policies and practices; the evolving 'global village' consciousness of the 1970-80s turned in 1990, into the enormous Indian market, and thereby became the ruling factor in the socio-political lives of Indians and ultimately the unrelenting determinant of their fate. However in the Bengali consciousness and inexhaustible cultural milieu, this so-called global village consciousness was especially active since the dawn of the connection between Bengali culture and Occidental knowledge.

In 1821, after Austria's Chancellor Metternich crushed the uprising in Naples, Rammohan Roy wrote, "I sincerely believe that the revolution of the common people of Naples is our own revolution. The enemies of freedom and friends of tyranny never have and never will achieve final success."[1]

In 1823, when three counties in South America declared armed rebellion against the Spanish Empire and won their nations' independence, Rammohan Roy ecstatically proclaimed, "Whatever be the differences in religion, race or language, freedom fighters of all the countries in the world are our friends."[2]

In 1820 when the people's revolution in Spain won temporarily, Rammohan sent then his congratulatory greetings. The grateful Spanish democrats dedicated the draft of their new constitution to their Indian friend Rammohan. When the July Revolution in France was successful in 1830, on his way to England, Rammohan boarded a French ship, saluted the French Revolution's flag, hugged the French sailors and joyfully shouted salutations to the Revolution again and again.[3]

Keeping aside the numerous facets of the Bengali International consciousness, one can find the century old advent of the global village consciousness in the brightest arena of Bengali literature. Published in 1887, Bankimchandra Chattopadhyay's book *Bibidha Prabandha — Prothom Bhag* includes an essay titled "Shakuntala, Miranda o Desdemona". Here Bankimchandra displayed unparalleled scholarship and wisdom in his comparative study of Kalidasa's heroine with Shakespeare's heroines Miranda from the comedy *The Tempest* and Desdemona from the tragedy *Othello*.[4]

While writing *Bhrantibilash* based on Shakespeare's *Comedy of Errors*, Ishwarchandra Vidyasagar wrote in the advertisement section, "After reading the comedy on mix-ups by the unrivalled poet Shakespeare of England, I thought if this tale composed in Bengali, it will entertain people. Accordingly, the episodes of this comedy are compiled in Bengali and named *Bhrantibilash*". Ishwarchandra also translated and published an anthology of 74 stories from the European popular fables by Aesop with the title *Kothamala*.[5]

The contemporary film is a testament to the popularity of Bibhutibhushan Bandopadhyay's novel *Chander Pahar* written in early 20th century about the adventures of Shankar in the remote Richtersveld mountain range of Africa.[6] In a number of novels written in 1934-1938 author Dhirendralal Dhar also spun tales of adventure in exotic settings like Africa. The 1935 Italian invasion of Abyssinia served as the setting for the novel *Abyssinia Fronte*.[7]

In 1936 after travelling abroad for the sixth time, High Court lawyer Dr. Saratchandra Basak wrote the book *Vu-Parjatan* citing the reason — "We have to leave home and find ourselves under the free skies. We have to awaken the thirst for the far away."[8]

In 1945 in the 'pujabarshiki' issue of Dev Sahitya Kutir's magazine *Alpona*, Premendra Mitra introduced his famous 'Ghanada' character in the story "Mosha" set in Sakhalin island, then a centre of conflict between Russia and Japan. Later in numerous stories Ghanada with the devotion of an explorer traversing latitudes and longitudes, from the

North to the South Pole, through remote jungles and fearsome volcanoes and various faraway corners of the world including the peak of the Everest, appeared in the role of a saviour of mankind.[9] In the brilliant Ghanada novel *Surjo Kandle Sona*, Mitra presented a close historical account of the Spanish conquest and plunder on Peru in 15th century South America.[10]

As the talented successors of this genre, Satyajit Ray's Professor Trailokeshwar Shanku and Adrish Bardhan's Professor Nut Boltu took curious Bengali readers on global explorations since the 1960s. First introduced in 1962 in *Sondesh* magazine, the Professor Shanku's character is much discussed in scholarly circles. Adrish Bardhan in the story "Rongin Kancher Jongol" in Professor Nut Boltu series explored highly imaginative science fiction horror where the fall of a star due to crystal storms in the Andromeda galaxy affects New York, Cambodia and Aravalli mountain range in India, as early as 1972.[11]

The newfound influence of international politics can be easily seen in the Bengali language. In 1920 and the first half of 1930, a number of Bengali books were published about Musollini that discussed Musollini's political ideology in the Italian social context and described the contemporaneous successes of the country. Simultaneously, texts on Socialism from Soviet Russia were smuggled in ships to Kolkata where they were translated in Bengali.

Since the 1980s onwards, the greatest treasures of world literature enriched Bengali translation literature. The poems of contemporary Turkish poet Nazim Hikmet found a permanent place in Bengali literature through the ingenious translations of Subhash Mukhopadhyay. Along with the rest of the world Bengali readers also got to read John Reeds thrilling account of the Russian Revolution, *Ten Days That Shook The World*, in the translated version *Duniya Kanpano Dos Din*. Nobel laureate Boris Pasternak's *Doctor Zhivago*, the controversial insider's account of Russia bloodied and agitated by the Revolution, was translated and published in Bengali as early as 1960.[12] Pavel Korchagin from Nikolai Ostrovsky's novel *How The Steel Was Tempered or Ispat*, and Gregor Melekov from Mikhail Sholokhov's Nobel winning novel *And Quiet Flows The Don or Dhir Probahini Don*, are beloved characters for the Bengali readers of 1960-70-80s.[13]

The Volunteers, American labour activist and leader Steve Nelson's heart-rending novel about the International Brigade of pro-democracy volunteers from all over the world in the 1936 Spanish civil war, was available to Bengali readers by 1983.[14] During this time, the Bengali readers were also perusing Erich Maria Remarque's novel about the horrifying cruelty of Nazi concentration camps, *Spark of Life*, or *Swopno Niye*, and Bruno Apitz's novel about Buchenwald concentration camp, *Naked Among Wolves*.[15]

While a prisoner at Gestapo prison Pankrác, Julius Fuêik the editor of the Daily Rudé Právo, mouthpiece of the Czechoslovakian Communist Party, wrote his diary *Notes From The Gallows* secretly in pencil on scraps of paper. In 1989 only Bengali readers witnessed this immortal tale of struggle against fascist torture that saw light of day after the end of the war and won the hearts of freedom loving people all over the world.[16] Such examples are numerous, inexhaustible and varied.

Innumerable international poems and songs of protest translated in Bengali, brought the global village consciousness to a permanent place in Bengali creativity and galvanized the Bengali rebel spirit. Songs like "Story of Four Rivers" composed in the atmosphere of worldwide mass uprisings of the 1970s, the song about labour leader Joe Hill from the copper mining community of South African province Natal, even the revolutionary songs of Mazzini and Garibaldi in the voices of protesting Bengalis during the 1970-1980s built the bridge of humanity over international borders.

In conclusion, it can be said with optimistic conviction that although the aggressive globalization of multinational corporations trying to capture the world's market overwhelmed India in the 1990s, true global village consciousness has a place under the vast liberal umbrella of Bengali culture and in the ideologically inclined thoughtful Bengali mindset even after traversing a century. At the centre of the flux of Bengali universal philosophy, there remains the ideal of "*Vasudhaiva Kutumbakam.*"

NOTES

1. Rammohan Roy's letter to Lord Buckingham, 11/08/1821.
2. *Monthly Repository of Theology and General Literature*, Vol. 18, p. 575.
3. Sibnath Sastri, *History of the Brahmo Samaj*, Vol. I.
4. "Shakuntala is the painting of a painter; Desdemona the lifelike sculpture of a sculptor. Shakuntala is half Miranda and half Desdemona. Mature Shakuntala is similar to Desdemona, innocent Shakuntala resembles Miranda", *Bankim Rachanabali*, Jogeschandra Bagal (ed.), Sahitya Sangsad, 1361, pp. 179-84.
5. "If reading *Bhranti Bilas* brings pleasure to even one person, I will feel that my labour is successful", *Vidyasagar Rachanabali*, Subodh Chakrabarty (ed.), Kamini Prokashonaloy, Kolkata, 1399.

6. *Chander Pahar*, Bibhutibhusan Bandopadhyay, 1st Aswin 1344, Kolkata.
7. Introduction to the novel *Abyssinia Fronte*, "In this age by the word civilization we understand European civilization. Although they were morally Christians, European statesmen prefer canons, bombs and poisonous gases over sacrifice, peace and service. The Abyssinian war is one such dark side of European civilization", *Adventure Omonibus*, Dhirendralal Dhar, Sahitya Bihar, Kolkata, 1393, pp. 194-295.
8. Countries included in the book — Myanmar, Malaysia, Singapore, Hong Kong, Japan, Switzerland, Yugoslavia, Turkey, Canada, Italy, Bulgaria, Austria, Poland, and various regions of Russia and America, *Vu-Porjoton*, Sen Brothers and Co., 15 College Square, Kolkata, 1937, Introduction + p. 268.
9. *Ghonada Somogro-1*, Premendra Mitra, Surojit Dasgupta (ed.), Ananda Publishers Pvt. Ltd., Kolkata, 2000, Introduction.
10. "Surjo Kandle Sona" published in book form in 1969 had the following advertisement on the title page — "The geographical expansion of this novel is from the Indian east coast, covering the lofty Andes on the far east coast of the Pacific Ocean to the Peru Empire. The time period covers the end of the fifteenth century to early decades of the sixteenth century. Many colourful names from history makes an appearance in this novel." *Ghonada Somogro-3* , Premendra Mitra, Surojit Dasgupta (ed.), Ananda Publishers Pvt. Ltd., Kolkata, 2000, Introduction.
11. "Rongin Kancher Jongol", *Purobi*, Deb Sahitya Kutir, Kolkata, 1379. Adrish Bardhan, "Professor Nut Boltu Chokro", Ananda Publishers Pvt. Ltd., Kolkata, 2008.
12. John Reed, *Duniya Kapano Dos Din*, Pragati Publishers, Moscow, 1967. Boris Pasternak, *Doctor Zhivago*, Rupa and Company, Kolkata 12, Buddhadeb Basu edited 1st Bengali edition, September 1960.
13. Nikolai Ostrovsky, *Ispat*, National Book Agency Pvt. Ltd., Kolkata. Mikhail Sholokhov, *Dhir Probahini Don*, National Book Agency Pvt. Ltd., Kolkata, 1959. "Sagore Milaye Don" (The Don Flows Home To The Sea) Part 1 (1958), Part 2 (1963), National Book Agency Pvt. Ltd., Kolkata.
14. Steve Nelson, *Volunteers*, Dipayan, Kolkata, 1983.
15. Erich Maria Remarque, *Swopno Niye (The Spark of Life)*, Nath Brothers, Kolkata, 1985.
16. Julius Fuêik, *Fanshir Moncho Theke*, National Book Agency Pvt. Ltd., Kolkata, 1989.

7

Globalization and Folk Art

Swapan Kumar Mandal

Globalization is an international situation that emerged at the end of the twentieth century in which the investment, employment, production and marketing systems of the world reached beyond the physical boundaries and expanded into the inter-state range. As a result, the whole world has become a wider society and various countries are simultaneously participating in the same investment, employment, production and marketing process.[1]

It is a mechanism of mutual interaction and interconnection that initiates coordination and interaction between governments, institutions and peoples of different nations. The driving force of this approach is international trade and investment, and its main supporting force is information technology. Environment, culture, political system, economic development and progress and human and social progress; It has a clear effect on everything.[2]

On the other hand, folk art encompasses all kinds of visual art created in the context of folk culture. There are many definitions of folk art, but generally objects have some kind of practical utility rather than merely decorative ones. The makers of folk art are usually trained through a popular tradition rather than a fine tradition of culture. This art created by grouped people who live in the structure of an advanced society but who are separated from the advanced genre of art for geographical or cultural reasons is considered as folk art.[3]

Folk art reflects the roots of a community's cultural life and way of life. They contain the traditional form of explicit culture associated with the field of folk arts and cultural heritage. Visible folk art incorporates historically created objects for use in a traditional community. Invisible folk art encompasses industries such as music, dance and narrative structure. In fact, both visible and invisible were developed to meet the needs of the time.[4]

Folk art is the traditional folk art of Bengal; Its origin is centred on religious and social needs. Various folk arts associated with social and religious events like Alpana, Manasaghat, Lakshmi Sara, Mangalaghat etc. Although religious passions are included in the document, it is considered a way of livelihood. Furniture and appliances adorned with various designs and ornaments meet the practical needs of the household. Used as a decoration for sports dolls, hobby watches, gold and silver jewelry. However, religious, social, cultural — all arts have some aesthetic appeal. Therefore, no matter how bitter the mask of a violent beast or monster is, a kind of juice is also known in the combination of a touch of the maker's hand and a tradition of traditional-reformation-traditional emotions.[5]

Folk art materials are very common. Various types of artifacts are made from locally available clay, wood, cloth, yarn, shoal, conch, tube, bamboo, cane, horn etc. Gold, silver, bronze, ivory and other valuable materials are also used. The machinery of folk art is also very common. Through these simple elements and machinery, Bengal folk artists have been making outstanding art for ages. Most of the professional-amateur artists associated with the industry live in the villages. Kamar, Kumar, carpenter, Patuya, Sonaru, Kansaru, Shankhari, Tantai and others are engaged in various artistic activities as artisans. These handmade industries are also a way to make a living. The artists in the alphabet and caricature are ordinary women in the household. They have no distinguished identity as an artist. In the rural area, there are more such fine artists who create a variety of toys, furniture and accessories from aesthetic consciousness.[6]

There are various methods of making folk art such as advanced industry. The divisions of folk art on materials and canvases are as follows:

1. *Painting and sketch:* Paintings, portraits, masks, wall paintings, tattoos and other mosaics, films, chronographs, hobbies, watches, nakshi dolls etc.;
2. *Embroidery:* Miscellaneous embroidery of kantha, handkerchief, sari and other clothing;
3. *Weaving:* Nakshi bandage, nakshi shika, nakshi fan, basket, flower garden;
4. *Modelling or replicating models:* Dolls and toys, watch-liners,

masks, moulds, nakshi pits, nakshi darmas, sweets, ornaments, boats, chariots, tazia, cot, couches, boxes, arks, pellets etc.;

5. *Engraving:* Engraving wood products, terracotta paintings, various metals;
6. *Inlaying:* Various ornaments of gems, pearls, diamonds and emeralds, ornamental decoration by coloured glass and stone.[7]

One of the heritage of Bengal is associated with folk art. But now, due to lack of technology, modernity and finances, this ancient art of village Bengal is gradually disappearing.[8] With the advent of modern technology, the whole world has become a village with globalization or urbanization. So we can say that the present era is the era of globalization, the present era is the era of renewal. In the wake of this era of change, folk-art is in crisis today. As technology has saved time in our lives in the advancement of science, it has made the distant closer. As a result, we have lost many things. Convenient sluggishness has made people fall in love with technology at the expense of nepotism, as well as losing its social, family, personal relationships. For which our traditional folk culture is in the throes of the folk art crisis. Our traditional rural folk-arts are in crisis today due to the pressure of modern technology on globalization.[9]

One of our traditional herds of rural living is folk-art. Once upon a time a cow car was the only transport vehicle. In the carriage of the cow, cargo was transported from one place to another, just as the cattle carriage was carried. We hear about the joy of getting married in a carriage with a grandmother; According to the story of the allegory we have. Again, how many song lyricists sing about this cow car. Okay carousel brother, how many robe am I on the sidewalk. "This caricature of music, as it is in crisis today, has taken the place of a petrol-diesel-powered engine motorbike in the spotless car; Which is polluting our green environment. It's like. The defeat of the art of the people, to the people, to life, to vision, to defeat."[10]

All the nations of the world admire Bengali cuisine. Where cooking takes place is commonly known as kitchen or pub. One of the culinary arts in this kitchen is the spice mill. From the birth of the Bengali nation, the tradition of this rock-pulse has been practiced since the birth of the Bengali nation. As a result of the condensation of spices in the usual rock, the friction of the rock-pulse reduced to the edge of the rock-smooth. Then the need to feed the rock-nest. And many of the artisans are making a living by doing this feeding or sharpening. Tired at noon the sun could not be heard in the sun when Kotani's shouting was cut off. But the Kotani's are cut off from the rock. At present, this shouting has been taken away from us. While many people run the world centred around this rock-kotany, the art-mindedness of the rock-kotani is hidden. These folk artists cheny, made by iron and hammer with various plants and leaves, fish pictures and fill the beauty of the smooth body of the shell. Where the artists worked perfectly. It is also a type of folk-art. Which is one of the brightest creations of folk culture. But under the pressure of modern technology, the circulation of rock-shoots in the verge of collapse of globalization is almost in crisis. Now the housewife is getting handmade packets of spices and various types of mixer machines are being replaced by shell shoots. To save time, guineas are naturally becoming interested in powdered spices and mixing machines. And for those who are leaving the kitchen in Bengali, shil-nora.

Alpana is another subject of folk art. This fantasy is an ancient tradition of ours, especially Bengalis. Imagination is used in the home for a long time. With the care of his mother, he drew the door of the dormant artist's mind in the backyard, on the floor of the house, drawing a variety of elegance. But this technique also did not escape the gravity of modern technology and globalization. We assume that some people are taking Alpana as a profession. But now he has used various materials as modern, modern context to take this folk art as a profession. Whose problem is — the pure destruction of folk culture and folk art. As we know it, folk art is a crop of folk culture's unique thinking, using modern sophisticated technology, the folk art is killing its individual artist. And this is where folk art is losing its independence by falling into the trap of modern technology. Thus, in the age of globalization, our traditional rural folk cultural cultures are facing a crisis today as modern technology is falling into the throes of gravity. The spirit of the folk society, the tension of the roots with the art of folk arts is eroding today. We are losing our past heritage, as we are losing our past, we are becoming lifeless by falling into the throes of modern technology, we are becoming mechanical by the day.

The centuries-old puppet dance art of Bengal has been in great distress during the globalization period. In good times, there were 63 doll parties in some places including Nadia's Dhankhali, Dhanatala. Now it has come to a minimum of twelve-fifteen. Tapan Kumar Biswas, head of the Folk Culture Department at Kalyani University, said,

> *"Because there is no future, no one wants to be associated with the industry. Even the families of artists are turning away. In love, some people still show doll dancing here and there. But what you earn doesn't fill your stomach."*[11]

Although, in the recent world, Folklore has been studied academically. Folklore today extends to a multidimensional branch of academia. Folklore has a close relationship with the various disciplines of literature, history, sociology, commerce, art, journalism, theatre, museums, urban planning and so on. This has brought new levels of analytical and scientific research to Folklore. Many new research horizons have been opened. In-depth analysis based on its socio-development by collecting various materials from Folklore is gaining ground. The role and importance of Folklore is being explored in various fields such as heritage preservation, reconstruction of history, achievement of human values, social development, preservation of environment, creation of industrial consciousness, urban planning, commercial propaganda etc. Folk-art is not just limited to collection, preservation and compilation, but research and analysis of the significance, role, and significance of folk art in various disciplines are of particular importance.[12]

One of the heritage of Bengal is associated with folk art. But now, due to lack of technology, modernity and finances, this ancient art of village Bengal is gradually disappearing. The State government has recently taken initiative to bring back the folk art of Bengal. In the interest of folk artists, 'Lok Prasar Yojana' has been launched in the state. Under this scheme, folk artists receive one-time allowance every month. Artists also get money for every public event. Apart from the government programmes, these folk artists participate in promoting various government projects. They are also given some money for it. Various academies have also been created to promote the culture of Bengal. A prize like Bangabhushan, Bangabibhushan has been introduced. But this opportunity is getting a few people of art. The rest of the society is not covered.[13]

So we can see both the consequences of globalization on folk art. But we need to emphasize the positive results and build a bridge between globalization and folk art. Only then will our folk art find a new way in the mix of heritage and modernity.

NOTES

1. https://bn.wikipedia.org/wiki/%E0%A6%AC%E0%A6%BF%E0%A6%B6%E0%A7%8D%E0%A6%AC%E0%A6%BE%E0%A6%AF%E0%A6%BC%E0%A6%A8 DATE:30.12.2019
2. https://bn.wikipedia.org/wiki/%E0%A6%AC%E0%A6%BF%E0%A6%B6%E0%A7%8D%E0%A6%AC%E0%A6%BE%E0%A6%AF%E0%A6%BC%E0%A6%A8 DATE:30.12.2019
3. Wertkin, Gerard C. (2004). "Introduction", in Wertkin, Gerald C. (ed.), *Encyclopedia of American Folk Art*, New York, London: Routledge, pp. xxvii-xxxiii.
4. https://en.wikipedia.org/wiki/Folk_art"cite_note-1
5. http://bn.banglapedia.org/index.php?title=%E0%A6%9A%E0%A6%BE%E0%A6%B0%E0%A7%81_%E0%A6%93_%E0%A6%95%E0%A6%BE%E0%A6%B0%E0%A7%81_%E0%A6%B2%E0%A7%8B%E0%A6%95%E0%A6%B6%E0%A6%BF%E0%A6%B2%E0%A7%8D%E0%A6%AA
6. http://bn.banglapedia.org/index.php?title=%E0%A6%9A%E0%A6%BE%E0%A6%B0%E0%A7%81_%E0%A6%93_%E0%A6%95%E0%A6%BE%E0%A6%B0%E0%A7%81_%E0%A6%B2%E0%A7%8B%E0%A6%95%E0%A6%B6%E0%A6%BF%E0%A6%B2%E0%A7%8D%E0%A6%AA
7. http://bn.banglapedia.org/index.php?title=%E0%A6%9A%E0%A6%BE%E0%A6%B0%E0%A7%81_%E0%A6%93_%E0%A6%95%E0%A6%BE%E0%A6%B0%E0%A7%81_%E0%A6%B2%E0%A7%8B%E0%A6%95%E0%A6%B6%E0%A6%BF%E0%A6%B2%E0%A7%8D%E0%A6%AA
8. https://bengali.oneindia.com/news/west-bengal/halsibagan-sarbojanin-focuses-on-bengal-s-abolishing-folk-art-042499.html
9. https://bhawaiya.blogspot.com/2019/10/blog-post.html
10. Do.
11. *Anandabazar Patrika*, 21 June, 2014.
12. https://archive.ittefaq.com.bd/index.php?ref=MjBfMDZfMjhfMTNfNF8yNF8xXzUxNjg3
13. https://bengali.oneindia.com/news/west-bengal/halsibagan-sarbojanin-focuses-on-bengal-s-abolishing-folk-art-042499.html

REFERENCES

Abanindranath Thakur, *Banglar Brata*, Calcutta, 1947.

Abinindranath Thakur, *Banglar Brata*, 1402, Biswabidyasangraha.

Ashok Mitra, *Bharater Chitrakala*, Part I, Ananda Publishars, 2000.

Dineshehandra Sen, *Brihat Banga*, Part I, Calcutta, 1934.

Golam Murshid, *Hazar Bachharer Bangla Sanskriti*.

Gurusaday Dutta, *Banglar Lokoshilpa o Lokonritya*, Chhatim Books, 2000.

Kalyanakumar Gangopadhyay, "Folklore in Bengal", *Banglar Lokoshilpa*, Kolkata Purogami Prakashani.

Mananjali Bandyopadhyay, *Banglar Alpana ebong Jaibabaichitra*, Essay in Jnan o Bijnan, August 2009, p. 400.

Rohini Kar, "Mirroring Aspirations: Ālpanas in the Brata Rituals of Bengal", *Remarking* (a Journal), Vol. II, Issue V, October, 2015.

8

Socio-economic Globalization
In Search of Among Santali People of West Bengal

Pinkan Biswas

Introduction

Indigenous people represent the ancient practices of lifestyle. In modern society, they are deprived from the modernity and also better lifestyle. Due to proper education, they are suffered from different problems in daily life. In Indian subcontinent, varieties of indigenous people are found in different places of the country. Santali is constitutionally affiliated language of a group of indigenous people residing basically in West Bengal.

Light needs to illuminate, to reach each corner, to enjoy itself by making happiness of the flora on the earth. All living components need light to grow, to be happy and also urge to make happy others. Indigenous people basically are known as tribes who had been following classical lifestyle to survive in this world. Scheduled Tribes (ST) are the constitutionally approved indigenous community of India; they basically are enlisted or scheduled as regards its unique culture and lifestyle respectively.[1]

In academics the word 'tribe' is used in anthropology as a conceptual category which refers to both as a 'type of society' (simple, egalitarian) and a 'stage' (devoid of centralized authority) in social evolution. In the Indian context, the anthropologists distinguished tribes as well as related them with the caste society in a continuum. To position 'Tribes' outside the state — and outside Indian society in general — is part of an until now influential anthropological debate on 'tribes' in India, which has explored, in particular, the level of integration of 'tribes' into wider society. It was the eminent Indian anthropologist Andre Béteille, who positioned tribes outside the control of the larger pre-colonial Indian states.[2] To counter this, Surajit Sinha has argued that tribes, as a dimension of a 'little tradition', cannot be adequately understood unless they are seen in relation to the 'great tradition' of Indian society.[3]

'Tribe' in India is also treated as an administrative category for the purpose of positive discrimination (e.g., reservation in jobs). Recently, the tribes in India are also viewed as 'indigenous people' or '*adivasis*' by the activists and social workers although the administrative category still seems to be important even to the tribes themselves.[4, 5]

The Santali people are an ethnic group native to India and Bangladesh in South Asia. Santali people are the largest tribe in the Jharkhand state of India in terms of population and are also found in the states of Assam, Bihar, Odisha and West Bengal. They have a sizeable population in Nepal and Bhutan. The Santals mostly speak Santali, an Austro-Asiatic language and that is the most widely-spoken of the Munda languages. Santal is most likely derived from a Bengali exonym. The term refers to inhabitants of Saont, now in the Midnapore region of West Bengal, the traditional homeland of the Santals.[6] Their ethnonym is Hor Hopon ("sons of mankind").[7]

The Santal are the third largest tribal communities of India after the Gond and the Bhil with a population over 4.26 million. They are largely distributed in the district of Balasore, Keonjhar, Mayurbhanj and Sundergarh of the state of Odisha and Paschim Mediniapur, Darjeeling, Jalpaiguri, Purulia, Burdwan of West Bengal. Olchiki is their mother tongue. Art, music and dance are highly prized in their culture. Their settled life has made them agricultural community as agriculture is their primary occupation. Their life is intimately connected with the forest and their economy. The community people live more or less in isolation with a very simple lifestyle. They face many problems relating to their day-to-day life as they are not getting healthy housing facility, proper sanitation facility, proper nutrition, safe drinking water, and other household amenities and so on. For improving their socio-economic conditions some of the basic services should adequately be provided. They need opportunities to develop their socio-economic status. There is a need to put more attention on educational aspects of Scheduled Tribes, where this only can motivate them for future life. The planners and policy-makers have to evolve suitable strategies and formulate relevant policies to enhance tribal development.

Socio-economic condition signifies an economic and social combined total measure of a person's work experience and of an individual's or family's economic and social position in relation to others; based on income, education and occupation. The tribal population is identified as the aboriginal inhabitants of our country.

It is a widely defined word with several connotations to many different people. There has been a hot debate about globalization. Some people believe globalization is a dangerous phenomenon which has changed the world in negative ways. To them, globalization has brought undesirable consequences to society, affecting its peace. On the other hand, another group of people regard globalization as a fruitful phenomenon, making the world more connected and informed than ever before. They look at it as a novel source for optimism in the world. It is clear that this group see various advantages of globalization.

Global education interconnects methods of teaching from worldwide systems to encourage the international development of environmental sustainability, as well as contribution towards fortifying global industries. These educational initiatives prioritize global access to school from the primary to the university levels, instigating learning experiences that prepare students for multinational leadership roles.

Globalization in education may end up creating more legitimate opportunities for a few advanced countries for a new form of colonization of developing countries.

It is important for the welfare of Santali people that the whole world have come to know about their culture. So it is the duty of every Indian that we give respects to the Santali culture like the other cultures and has to try to preserve it.

Socio-economic Condition of Santali Community

Indigenous communities of India are commonly referred to as tribal or *adivasi* communities and are recognized as Scheduled Tribes under the Constitution of India. Although the Constitution does not define Scheduled Tribes as such, it designates these communities as those which are scheduled in accordance with Article 342 of the Constitution. According to Article 342 of the Constitution, the Scheduled Tribes are the tribes or tribal communities or part of or groups within these tribes and tribal communities which have been declared as such by the President through a public notification. The criteria followed for specification of a community, as Scheduled Tribe are indications of primitive traits, distinctive culture, geographical isolation, shyness of contact with the community at large, and backwardness. At present, 533 tribes in India have been notified under Article 342 of the Constitution.

The population of STs in India as per 2011 Census was 10,42,81,034 constituting 8.61 per cent of the total population. The tribal population of India and West Bengal had grown at the rate of 17.64 per cent and 13.93 per cent during the period of 2001-2011 respectively. According to 2011 Census, the Scheduled Tribe population of West Bengal is 5.29 millions, which constitute 5.80 per cent of the total population and is unevenly distributed in the districts. Paschim Mediniapur has the highest 16.61 per cent tribal concentration in the state. Jalpaiguri district has 13.81 per cent, Purulia 10.21 per cent, Burdwan 9.24 per cent and Darjeeling district has 7.50 per cent, standing they are second, third, fourth and fifth respectively. More than 57 per cent of the Scheduled Tribes are concentrated in these districts. The lowest proportion of tribal population is in Kolkata district (0.20%). Other districts, viz. Howrah (0.28%), Cooch Behar (0.34%) and Purba Mediniapur (0.53%) could not reach even 1 per cent of total Scheduled Tribes population in the state. According to the 2011 Indian Cencus, majority of the Santal's from Jharkhand follow Hinduism at 54 per cent, with 37 per cent following "other religions and persuasions", mainly Sarna Dharam. Christianity is practised by 8.3 per cent present of the population. Islam, Sikhism, Buddhism and Jainism are followed by less than 1 per cent of the population. (ST-14 Scheduled Tribe Population By Religious Community — Jharkhand, census.gov.in. Retrieved 3rd November, 2019). The population of Scheduled Tribes has marginally increased in 2011 compared to 2001 Census whereas literacy rate has beefed up by 11.86 per cent and 14.5 per cent in India and West Bengal respectively.[8, 9]

Socio-economic Status (SES) is a combined measure of an individual's or family's economic and social position in relation to others, based on income, education, and occupation. For analyzing SES of a family, the household income, education, and occupation were examined, as well as combined income of the family members with other attributes were assessed. Socio-economic Status (SES) is often measured as a combination of education, income and occupation. SES, here, is sum total of the scores of family monthly income, and holding, dwelling housing, properties including furniture, luxurious items and other impediments.

Restoring land and livelihoods, empowering women, providing basic civic amenities such as fuel, water and sanitation are preconditions to advancements of rights of tribal children. Unless the government undertakes urgent steps to address these issues, its proclamations on child rights would remain examples of empty rhetoric and its actions would effectively continue to exclude those already sidelined. Following the increasing gap between the rich and the poor in the country, the gap between the tribal and non-tribal children is also widening rapidly, thereby further isolating the isolated. Respecting their claims at the outset should set the ball rolling in the right direction.

Globalization in Education

According to the Ministry of Human Resource Development Report of India (2004-05), the dropout rate among tribals in India from class I to X is 79 per cent. In the states of West Bengal and Jharkhand, both of which have substantial Santal populations, the rate is even higher: 88 per cent and 89 per cent, respectively. The figures suffice to gauge where tribals stand with regard to education. There are several provisions in India's Constitution designed to raise the educational level of tribals. These include free and compulsory education for all until the age of fourteen. The educational difficulties faced by tribals have been addressed through bilingual or multilingual programmes that start with education in the child's mother tongue, then transit to the regional or state language, and finally progress to the study of English. This three-language formula, however, remains in an experimental stage, and its practice is limited to isolated pilot projects.

The challenges of tribal education are daunting. There are 418 different tribes in India, with even more languages and dialects. Each group is also associated with a specific region through language, food habits, occupational characteristics and geography. To accommodate these diverse and culturally distinct communities with a single educational policy is a mammoth task, verging on the impossible.

The live and livelihood condition of the tribal people living in the Naxalite prone villages are more deplorable as compared to the national and state averages of the tribal people in India. The deplorable socio-economic conditions and apathy of state apparatus has created discontent among the tribals and the Naxalite problem is an upshot of socio-economic problems and governance deficit of state apparatus. Because of non-existence of market and state activities the 'development' is completely ramshackle in these tribal villages and it has provided a platform to the naxalite to operate their nefarious activities in these villages detached from the mainstream.[10]

One of the main problems in Santal education is the conflict between the state's policy of assimilating minorities into the mainstream culture and the tribal people's reluctance to abandon their identity. Santal children face a severe dilemma when they are forced to reject their own culture and accept schools' middle-class values. This conflict results in high dropout rates, low educational aspirations and degraded self-esteem.

The primary goal of formal education boils down to getting a salaried job through competitive examinations. The Santals, however, live with minimal commodity requirements. Their concept of pleasure differs from the mainstream. They have hardly any urge to compete for success. Santal life is not marked by the sense of formal discipline and punctuality that schools require both at the individual and the family levels. The Santals' village culture gives more scope for moving around at random than is typical of mainstream Bengali life. Hunting, fishing, roaming, drinking, singing and dancing all play a role.

Other problems lie in the medium of instruction, the curriculum, the method of evaluation, a lack of quality teaching and a defective administration. Everything seems set up against Santal children. For example, school tends to become painful for children when faced with a teacher who does not understand Santali and who speaks in a language the children do not understand. Children have to memorise lessons without understanding them. They become bored and, instead of going to school, prefer to look after the family's cows or goats.

Most teachers are from non-Santal communities. They hail from a middle-class background and are hardly aware of the socio-cultural life-world of the children. This lack of understanding creates serious problems.

Scheme for Construction of Hostels for ST Girls and Boys by the Ministry of Tribal Affairs, Government of India:

> The objective of the scheme is to promote literacy among tribal students by providing hostel accommodation to such ST students who would otherwise have been unable to continue their education because of their poor economic condition and the remote location of their villages. The Scheme was revised with effect from 1st April, 2008.
>
> An amount of ₹ 59.89 crore was spent till 31st December, 2012 against the Budget allocation of ₹ 78 crore during 2012-13.[11]

From the observations of educational scenario at the village, it is manifested that educational inclusion, access and enrolment of tribal children in the studied villages is inadequate. Even after introduction of several imperative measures from government, still villagers are facing several obstacles towards fearless educational attainment. The reasons which are thoroughly discussed above nevertheless denote their (of tribals) backwardness in education. The observations illustrated that lack of proper infrastructure and economic inability of the villagers towards education cost are also other reasons for marginalized education.[12]

In tribal world, especially among tribal women, education has always been considered less concerned due to excessive pressure of maintaining daily means of subsistence. Besides this, overdependency on some of the superstitions and ill cultural beliefs, such as witchcraft further have deteriorated the overall condition of tribal women society. In this study, evidences confirmed that economic backwardness leads to poor educational standard among the tribal women of the selected communities of Puruliya district. In this context, B.D. Dani (1979) wrote, "poverty and lack of education are very closely related . . . the social and geographical isolation of the tribal communities is the cardinal factor responsible for the slow progress of education among them."[13]

Educational Aspiration

Education is considered as the minimum necessity of life and the most influential agent of development. Further, education is also regarded as "a critical input for economic and social development. This is crucial for building human capabilities and widening the horizon of opportunities."[14]

Political and economic struggles must continue, but they must be underlined by tribal vision and their cultural values. Here education has to play a crucial and key-role to enable the tribal individual, and the tribal communities to overcome their mental and moral tension in the present cultural crisis. On the principle, education must be education for life and not for earning livelihood alone by right or wrong means and methods. That is to say, the cultural values of the tribals, which are also universal human values must be transmitted from one generation to another. Learning by doing or learning by work experience should replace the purely theoretical and intellectual information gathering exercises. The body, mind and spirit must get involved in the process of education from junior through intermediate and senior stages of education.

Educational institutions must become a part of social life in the village community and should not remain just an appendage to life, it must become practical source and centre of individual and community life. The formal, non-formal dichotomy in education process should be broken down with respect to tribal education in India.

The Government and the people in the plains have to forget about the dream of assimilation of tribals into the mainstream of Indian culture. The dehumanizing processes predominant in the so-called mainstream including the present unsatisfactory state of affairs in educational institutions and departments have to be completely discarded and disowned by the tribals. They have their tribal vision of life and live by their cultural values and defend their identity and promote it even in the midst of the onslaughts of modern culture. This is the valuable contribution that the tribal people of India want to offer at the feet of mother India to build up a mosaic of cultural panorama in this land.

The Government pays lip-service with regard to promoting the above educational programmes. The community is taking time to study and understand the intention behind such efforts as the people have been cheated by our own people in the past.

Primary, secondary and higher educational institutions have to be established and run by the communities with the above ideas and programmes in mind.

Tribal education must include business and commerce as an integral part of their education. Besides vocational education, cultural orientation towards business among the tribals is a must in saving the identity in the face of the economic onslaughts of the model world.

Many potential physical, mental, and social gifts with which the tribal people are endowed must be scientifically explored and given scope for development. Education must be made relevant to those gifts and natural talents and not *vice versa*. Physical fitness of tribal youth, care of children and sick by women teachers and nurses belonging to tribal communities must be brought up to national and international standards. These and other cultural heritages must be incorporated and used in planning for tribal education now and in the future. The immediate and distant cultural neighbours have to take up the challenge to cooperate and participate in this great and glorious venture of defending and promoting tribal identity through relevant meaningful education in India.

Santal parents' awareness towards the education of their children is positive. Santal parents prefer hostel (*ashram*) school. Poverty, transportation problem and fear of elephant are the main cause behind the irregularity of students to their school. Educated unemployment is very much prominent among the Santals in the studied area. Most schools remain open during the Santal festivals in the studied area as a result most of the Santal students do not attend their school during this period or on that day. About 62.5 per cent Santal students have private tuition teachers in the studied area. They expressed their need of special coaching classes in school or at hostel. History, Bengali and Geography is top most favourite subjects among the Santal students in the studied area. Mathematics and English is tough most subjects among the student in the studied area. About 27.5 per cent Santal students of this area do not get any type of scholarship. Students who are hosteller are unsatisfied to the menu, cleanness and hygiene at hostel. The literacy rate among the Santal is satisfactory but the attainment of higher education among the Santal population in the studied area is alarmingly very low and most educated santals are unemployed.[15]

Suggestions

Educational facilities are to be improved in the tribal areas to eradicate illiteracy. In this context, government schools to be strengthened as tribal children mostly depend on them. School drop-outs be discouraged through incentives and by creating interest in education.

Non-tribal exploitation should be stopped and government intervention should increase. The tribal development agencies should take care of development of tribes in the socio-economic spheres.

Non-Government hospitals are to be provided with infrastructure facilities and doctors to protect the tribal's health from the private practitioners and local curators.

Pre-natal and post-natal care and child care are to be impressed upon the tribal women of Anganwadi centres and health workers. Child mortality is to be reduced through immunization programmes and nutritious food to the lactating mothers.

Agriculture is to be given a new thrust in the tribal areas as more than 70 per cent depend on them. At the same time, non-agricultural wage employment through government programmers like NREGA be increased which would improve the economic conditions of the tribes thereby, get livelihood.

Conclusion

Article 46 of the Constitution of India provides that "the state shall promote with special care the educational and economic interests of the weaker sections of the people, and in particular of the Scheduled Castes and Scheduled Tribes and shall protect them from social injustice and all forms of exploitation." Thus, the Constitution of India gives due recognition to the problems and aspirations of the tribals. The policy of reservation forms the central part of the social justice dispensation of the Constitution. Reservation is meant to compensate for the unprecedented discrimination perpetrated against them from antiquity thereby empowering and integrating them with the mainstream society. The global initiative of placing people at the centre of development can proceed with added force through the empowerment of the peripheral socio-economic groups, especially the tribals.

The socio-economic development achieved in the tribal front has been most uneven between and within tribes. And even within a tribe a small elite has developed. "It is clear that all the gains of development have not reached the intended class and have been usurped by the better off in many cases." This phenomenon has resulted in the widening of the gap between the better off and worse off sections of the same tribe. In India, we do not "have a comprehensive social security net, for want of resources, for want of a system of management, and, therefore, governments have to play a very important role to fill the gap. This function is exercised mainly in the form of organizing activities directed at providing employment to those who are unable to find gainful work for want of skills and access to resources." An overall increase in the capabilities of the people is the primary objective of development. The intervention of the government is very much required in this field.

Therefore, government policies, programmes and schemes should take involvement of tribes to develop their socio-cultural, economic and health conditions in present day scenario by following transparency, participation and accountability criteria. And also promote both the welfare and development of the tribal people.

NOTES

1. Bapi Mishra, *Educational Awareness of Tribal People (Santali) in Malda District, West Bengal*, 2014, Volume 2, Issue 3, p. 630.
2. Béteille, A., "The Concept of Tribe with Special Reference to India", *European Journal of Sociology*, 1986, 27, pp. 297-318.
3. Sinha, S., "Tribal Cultures of Peninsular India as a Dimension of Little Tradition in the Study of Indian Civilization: A Preliminary Statement", *Journal of American Folklore*, July-September, 1958, 71, pp. 504-18.
4. Xaxa, V., "Tribes as Indigenous People of India", *Economic and Political Weekly*, 1999, 34(51):3589-3595.
5. Xaxa, V., "Transformation of Tribes in India: Terms of Discourse", *Economic and Political Weekly*, 1999, 34(24):1519-1524.

6. Chulte-Droesch, Lea Verfasser, *Making Place through Ritual: Land, Environment and Region among the Santal of Central India*, 2018, ISBN 978-3-11-053973-8, OCLC 1054397811.
7. Somers, George E., *The Dynamics of Santal Traditions in a Peasant Society*, Schenkman Pub. Co., 1979, OCLC 5668202.
8. *Census of India*, Office of the Registrar General and Census Operation, Ministry of Home Affairs, Government of India, New Delhi, India, 2001.
9. *Census of India*, Office of the Registrar General and Census Operation, Ministry of Home Affairs, Government of India, New Delhi, India, 2011. *Tribal Profile at a Glance 2014.*
10. Dung Dung, K., Pattanaik, B.K., "Lives and Livelihood of Tribals in Naxalite Affected Villages: A Study in Sundergarh District of Odisha", *Asian Journal of Social Sciences & Humanities*, 2013; 2(4):94-107.
11. *Annual Report 2012-2013*, from Ministry of Tribal Affairs, Government of India, p. 126.
12. Subhandu Patra and Nilakantha Panigrahi, *Educational Status of the Marginalized: A Study among the Santals of Paschim Medinipur District, West Bengal*, GoI: 10.31901/24566756.2018/57.1-3.2220, PRINT: ISSN 0971-8923 ONLINE: ISSN 2456-6756, J Soc Sci, 57(1-3): 22-28 (2018).
13. Dani, B.D., "Tribal Education: Problems of Today and Tomorrow: A study of Buska Tribe of Uttar Pradesh", Cited in H.C. Upadhyay (ed.), *Scheduled Caste and Scheduled Tribes in India: A Socio-economic Profile*, Anmol Publications, pp. 227-28.
14. Tripathy, S.N., *Literacy for Tribal Women*, Abhijeet Publications, Delhi, p. 15.
15. Nizamuddin Ahmed and Swami Tattwasarananda, *Education of Santals of Jhargram: An Ethnographic Study*, 2018, p. 58; p-ISSN: 2279-0845; Volume 23; Issue 7; Ver 3; DOI: 10.9790/0837-2307035158; Address: www.iosrjournals.org

9

Globalization
Its Effect on Indian Society and Youth

Shashanka Sekhar Roy

Globalization is a concept of economic integration and political interaction. It establishes the connection between countries and people around the world. It can build financial and commercial transactions, spread cultural aspects among the entire planet to overcome global problems. Globalization indeed constitutes integration of national economies into the international economy through trade, direct foreign investment, short term capital flows, international flows of workers and humanity generally, end flows of technology (Bhagwati, 2004).[1] Globalization refers to how more people connected across larger distances. They create a new society in which they do more similar thinking, affect each other's lives more deeply, follow more or the same norms and grow more awareness of what they share. Government, also have played an important role in the determination of levels of income, savings, investments and employment in the society (Naidu, 2006).[2] We can say that the term globalization means International Integration in all aspects (Beck, 2018).[3]

Globalization has been dominating the world since the nineties of the last century. The wave of globalization hit India at the end of the last century and still, the country is flowing with the current global changes. The term globalization used to describe different countries joining to think about themselves as a part of the world rather than as separate countries. It has four parameters permitting the free flow of goods by removing or reducing trade barriers between two countries, creating an environment for the flow of capital between two countries, allowing the free flow of technology transfer and creating an environment for the free movement of labour, between the countries of the world

(Ahuja, 1992).[4] Indian economy had experienced major policy changes in the early 1990s. The new economic reform, popularly known as, Liberalization, Privatization and Globalization (LPG model) aimed at making the Indian economy the fastest growing economy and globally competitive (Agrawal, 2014).[5] Globalization describes how different world cultures, population and economies are interdependent on each other. It is the consequence of cross-border business, technology, goods, investments, information and services along with the labour market are the most popular components of such activity. Though nations have established world-wide integration over many centuries ago by enabling political, economic and social partnerships today, the same endeavour has improved due to innovations and intensified transportation.

The world now became a global village which makes distance even shorter, making the cultural and economic relations easier, more efficient and faster. It develops among other activities, actions such as protection and promotion of the human rights, internal interchange of young people, the action of information, spreading and sensitization of public opinion, collaboration in the emergency humanitarian assistance and participation. Globalization can bring countless advantages to young people. They are standing a sharp end of the globalization and be considered key agents of change for globalization, as well as its potential victims. The youth represent the most dynamic and vibrant segments of the population. India is one of the youngest nations in the world, with about 65 per cent of the population under 35 years of age. The youth in the age group of 15-29 years comprise 27.5 per cent of the population (MYAS, 2019-2020).[6] Now, the question is what globalization means to the young people and what is the impact of it has had on their lives?

International Labour Office, University of Washington and UNICEF identified some key issues as relevant areas where globalizing is most significantly affecting young people (United Nations, 2001).[7] These key issues are —

- Access to and privatization of education.
- Young people's access to technology.
- Globalization of youth activism and human rights.
- Global youth culture and youth identity.
- Export oriented manufacturing industries and young workers.
- HIV/AIDS prevention, treatment and care for youth.
- Indigenous youth.
- The vulnerability of agricultural youth.

- Violence and young people's security.
- Trafficking of young women.

Some Positive Impacts of Globalization on Indian Society and Youth

Impact on Education

Youth Policy of India, 2014[8] describes, to create a productive youth workforce that contributes to economic development; the youth must be educated and equipped with the necessary skill-set to forge sustainable livelihoods. India is one of the leading developing countries. Globalization has a great impact on students. India needs to specialization and promotion of higher education in the country. Most developed countries have advanced schools, colleges and universities. They encourage pupil from overseas to study there.

Impact on Technology and Jobs

Globalization has increased the speed of communication. In recent times, social media has made world distance insignificant. The integration of technology in India has transformed jobs, which required specialized skills, such as numerical, analytical, communication and interactive skills. India is obtaining a worldwide recognition and slowly moving towards to become a significant economic, political and technological strength. Globalization has resulted in growing global markets in services. People can now execute trade services globally — from medical advice to software writing to data processing that was not possible before globalization (Agarwal, 2019).[9]

Globalization made job opportunity for young people across the globe as per their requirement and quality. The advent of foreign companies and growth in the economy has led to job creation. It means encouraging nations to specialize and produce plenty of goods available in their local market. However, these jobs are concentrated more in the services sector and this has led to the rapid growth of the service sector. Globalization declined the gap between the rich and the poor through job opportunity of everyone by their choice. Foreign investment can develop the economy of developing countries by giving financial assistance and establishing industry. Globalization encourages nation to specialize and produce plenty of goods available in the local market. Now, the different countries produce different products and what is most important and surprising that no country is self-sufficient. The larger the market is, the more the returns.

Impact on Youth Culture and Health

Each country has its own heritage of culture incorporating all countries form a global one was very tough before globalization. Through globalization people get to know what is happening in other countries by media cover events of other countries. Human rights can work worldwide where necessary. It can better access of knowledge. Make communication with other young people from all around the world. That can reduce racism. People today especially the young develop an identity that gives them a sense of belonging to a worldwide culture, which includes an awareness of events, practices, styles and information that are a part of the global culture. Media such as television and especially the Internet, which allows for instant communication with any place in the world, play an important part in developing a global identity. When people have the chance to communicate with each other, they can also understand the other cultures better, become more tolerant and more open to what surrounds them (Chinnammai).[10]

Some Adverse Socio-Cultural Effects on Indian Youth and Society

Cross-border competitions, terrorism, job insecurities, price instability, environmental consequences, conflict among states and currency fluctuations are a big threat, which forced to remove people from their homes. While economic prosperity may offer an incised opportunity for some, the benefits are not available to all.

Education

Globalization has aided in the explosion of information on the web that has helped in greater awareness among people. The advent of private education, coaching classes and paid study material has created a gap between the haves and have-nots. It has become increasingly difficult for an individual to obtain higher education. Sometimes, there is also the possibility of sub-standard courses offered to the students, which may mislead innocent citizens of India. This will only lead to social tensions. Globalization and commercialization of education have thus become a reality. India is witnessing a new era in the field of Management Education. The entire higher education in India has been thrown into a dangerous situation, which was never witnessed before. The World Bank has published a report on higher education in developing countries, titled 'Peril and Promise'. Is there any doubt, however, that the current drive of globalization of higher education will not bring any promise to developing countries; on the contrary, it will thrust into a catastrophic peril the higher education system in developing countries? (Swar & Pandey, 2008).[11]

Culture and Society

Indian has a high heritage of culture, which contains moral and eternal values. However, globalization is about to destroy this. Indian Classical music has gained worldwide recognition but recently, Western music is too becoming very popular in our country. Western dance forms such as Jazz, Hip-hop, Salsa, and Ballet have become common among Indian youngsters. The Western influence of individualism has led to an inspirational generation of youth. Concepts of national identity, family, job and tradition are changing rapidly and significantly. There is greater access to news, music, movies, and videos from around the world. Foreign media houses have increased their presence in India. It has a psychological, social and cultural influence on our society and youth. It can be seen with the rise of big businesses, which have nearly killed the small traditional businesses in our society. Consumerism has permeated and changed the fabric of contemporary Indian society. Western fashions are coming to India. The traditional Indian dress is increasingly being displaced by Western dresses especially in urban areas. Media, movies and serials set a stage for patterns of behaviour, dress codes.

Globalization does not have any positive impact on agriculture. The international norms imposed by WTO and other multilateral organizations have reduced government support for agriculture. This has increased the vulnerability of Indian farmers. Farmers are also increasingly dependent on seeds and fertilizers sold by the MNCs, which triggered off some detrimental effects on society. The city-centric services sector and job creation have led to an increase in rural to urban migration. It will bring imbalance to Indian society and youth. Although, the last decade came to be known for its jobless growth, as job creation was not proportionate to the level of economic growth.

Conclusion

The impact of globalization on our Indian society and youth is mixed.

We should check Western culture, education, economy before accepting to preserve the rich culture and diversity of India. Indian youth are the majority in the world and society made with high bonding among each other. Western does not mean always good. Youth has to judge before recognizing any thing. Thus, this assignment can conclude that though, globalization has some negative results; it has some positive effects on Indian youth and society.

NOTES

1. Bhagwati Jagdish, *In Defence of Globalization*, Oxford University Press, 2004.
2. Naidu, Y. Gurappa, "Globalization and its Impact on Indian Society", *IPSA*, 2006, Vol. 67, No. 1, p. 1.
3. Beck, U., *What is Globalization?*, John Wiley & Sons, 2018.
4. Ahuja, Ram, *Social Problem in India*, Rawat Publication, Jaipur, 1992.
5. Agrawal, Rinku, "Globalization and its Effect on India", *Economic Affairs*, Vol. 59, S Issue, 2014, pp. 797-803.
6. *Annual Report (2019-20)*, Ministry of Youth Affairs and Sports, Government of India, New Delhi.
7. United Nations, *Report on the World Social Situation*, accessed May 2001.
8. *National Youth Policy, 2014*, Ministry of Youth Affairs and Sports, Government of India, New Delhi.
9. Agarwal, Ritu, "The Effects of Globalization on Indian Society and Culture", March 27, 2019, Vol. 61, Issue 2.
10. Chinnammai, S., *Effect of Globalization on Education and Culture*, New Delhi.
11. Swar Biranchi Narayan and Pandey, Shikha, "Impact of Globalization on Higher Education", *Researchgate*, 2008.

10

Bengal Culture
On Special Reference to the thoughts about Bratachari

Soniya Majumder

Globalization is the process of interaction and integration among people, companies and governments worldwide. Globalization has accelerated since the 18th century due to advances in transport and communication technology. The increase in global interaction has caused a growth in international trade and the exchange of ideas and culture. It is primarily an economic process of interaction and integration that is associated with social and cultural aspects. Globalization affects every part of human life. Cultural globalization refers to the transmission of ideas, meaning and values around the world in such a way as to extend and intensify social relation. This process is marked by the common consumption of cultures that have been diffused by the internal, popular culture media and international travel, but there are a number of negative impacts globalization has on cultural diversity, including the influence multinational corporations have on promoting a consumer culture, exploitation of workers and markets and influencing societal values. This promoters a homogeneous set of values and beliefs.

In the same way from the late nineteenth century onwards, middle-class Bengali men displayed major anxieties regarding the declining health of their 'race'. This came at a time when a colonial discourse of 'effeminate' come to the Bengali and Bengalis — especially the English-educated middle class — responded by constructing a counter-discourse that itself was marked by a profound ambivalence. Each individual and each race or nation have their "own rhythm" which is often reflected through their performing arts, but in those days Bengali lost their own specific 'rhythm', they would suffer dire consequences of becoming extinct. In those days Bengali '*Bhadrolok*' society was accepted a new type of culture which called '*Adhunatan*' or 'Modern' culture. Mainly educated Bengali middle class society mostly accepted this and forgot their own rhythm.[1]

This became manifest in the astonishing growth of physical cultural institutes in various shapes and sizes. Even though there were different ideologies and techniques that moulded this world of physical culture, they were shaped by the same premise regarding the corporal body and health-related anxieties of the middle-class Bengali. The Bratachari movement was no different in this respect, although its uniqueness lies in the fact that the movement combined physical exercises with a few specific dance forms. The founder of the movement, Gurusaday Dutta (1882-1941), claimed that the Bratachari movement was fashioned on the 'authentic folk traditions' of Bengal and was thus more suitable for Bengalis than other forms of exercise, especially colonial sports like cricket and football. This article seeks to examine Dutta's principles of selection for choosing certain specific 'folk traditions' for the movement, and to demonstrate the global influences that shaped his construction of an avowedly indigenous movement.

Gurusaday Dutta, who was a civil servant, folklorist and writer. He was the founder of the Bratachari Movement in the 1930s. He was born in 1882 in Birasri, Karimganj, Assam province, British India. He completed his Entrance examination at Government College, Sylhet where he stood first in 1898. He stood second in the F.A. Examination from Presidency College in 1901 and was awarded the Scindia Gold Medal. In 1905, he passed the Indian Civil Service examination. He was District Magistrate and also the Government Chief Whip in the Bengal Legislative Council. In his youth, he started to take active interest in social service and participated in helping fire-fighters and assisting in relief work. He was one of the social reformers of the first half of the nineteenth century who thought independently about various avenues of service to the rural poor. In 1918, he started the first Rural Reconstruction Movement in Birbhum, India. He then extended the movement to several districts where he was subsequently posted, like Bankura, Howrah and Mymensingh. In his working period he was influenced by Rabindranath Tagore very deeply. In 1931, he met Cecil Sharp, who was a folk dance revivalist. He also attended All-England Folk Dance & Folk Song Festival.[2] This inspired him to do something for Bengali culture. When he visited Japan, he saw how Japanese were respected their own rhythm of culture, after his inspiration. He founded Bratachari movement in 1930s in colonial Bengal. Bratachari was a movement for spiritual and social improvement in India. The movement aimed to raise the self-esteems and national awareness of people of undivided India regardless of their religion, caste, sex or age. It was a comprehensive programme of physical, mental and intellectual culture, based on folk traditions of physical exercise, art, dance, drama, music, singing and social service. The Bratachari undertakes to perform good deeds, strengthen fellowship and develop the mind and body through dance. Dutta was in essence attempting to construct a 'martial' genealogy for Bengalis through the revival of adequately 'masculine', 'indigenous' folk dance forms. What emerges as particularly interesting is Dutta's emphasis on the authenticity of folk traditions, as well as the basic anxieties at play behind the drive to revive a singular folk tradition.

From a distance, the Bratachari movement might appear as a mere physical improvement regime, with a few 'folk' elements thrown in, and a corresponding social reconstruction programme. However, the movement was far more nuanced than at first meets the eye. Thus, through the use of 'folk' song and dance, Gurusaday Dutta aimed at inventing a tradition which eventually would lead to the building of a nation in the not-so-distant future. This idea of using what he called an 'authentic folk tradition' for the creation of a stronger 'race' becomes quite clear from his writings.

Bratachari Movement: The Structure

The structure and ideology of the Bratachari movement was dictated by a series of oaths or ***bratas***. The oaths were structured by five basic principles: **Knowledge, Labour, Truth, Unity** and **Joy**. In order to transform these lofty ideals into practice, Gurusaday Dutta also specified sixteen ***pons*** (promises) that needed to be practised in daily life. These vows were programmatic and comprehensive:

1. Extending the bounds of knowledge.
2. Banishment of jungles and weeds.
3. Enhancing the dignity of labour.
4. Cultivation of vegetables and fruits.
5. Free circulation of light and air.
6. Care of cattle.
7. Maintaining the purity of water.
8. Observance of tidiness.

9. Promotion of physical exercise and play.
10. Emancipation of women.
11. Earning before marrying (for women *bratacharis*, this vow was changed to gentle and modest behaviour).
12. Pursuit of crafts and industries.
13. Observance of punctuality.
14. Dedication of self to service.
15. Developing the spirit of Fellowship and Equal Citizenship.
16. Promotion of the spirit of Joy.[3]

In addition to these primary vows, there were some additional vows and restrictive injunctions that the *bratacharis* had to abide by, and included:

17. Avoidance of waste.
18. Conservation along with progress.
19. Obedience to the leader.
20. Development through self-sacrifice.
21. Cleanliness in thought, word and deed.
22. Smartness of behaviour.

There was a set of restraints or prohibitions, which themselves are more revealing of Dutta's project:

1. I will not hang the *knocha*.[4]
2. I will not speak in a mixed language.[5]
3. I will not develop a *paunch*.
4. I will not eat except when hungry.
5. I will not spend beyond my earnings.
6. I will not give way to fear before dangers or obstacles.
7. I will not indulgc in luxury.
8. I will not show anger even when angry.
9. I will not forget to smile even in misfortune.
10. I will not be puffed up with pride.
11. I will not be untrue in thought and spirit.
12. I will not be discourteous in manner.
13. I will not place reliance in luck, chance or destiny.
14. I will not rest without striving.
15. I will not flee from failure.
16. I will not beg for a livelihood.
17. I will not violate the given word.

Further, there were four promises that were denoted by the syllables in the word ***Bra-ta-cha-ri***.

Bra — Brata — Ideal:
We take the *Brata* to serve Bengal;
Along with Bengal, to serve Bharat;
Along with Bharat, to serve the world or Humanity.

Ta — Tarunata — Youthfulness:
We shall bring the living stream of youthfulness into our lives.

Cha — Chai — Desire
We desire a strong body and a free and liberal mind.

Ri — Ritimoto — Systematically:
We shall systematically endeavour to pursue the vows.[6]

Apart from these formal vows, there were different vows suitable for different age groups, for example, for small children and young boys and girls until they were mature enough to formally become a *bratachari*. Whoever chose to abide by the sixteen main vows came to be known as a *bratachari*. Apart from the vows and the restrictive injunctions, there were also sixteen 'acts' which every *bratachari* had to perform regularly, better known as '*alis*', according to the terminology used in the movement.[7] The main 'acts' were as follows:

1. *Abrittali* — the act of recitation of the above mentioned vows and restrictive injunctions.
2. *Krityali* — the act of working (performing good deeds).
3. *Sangeetali* — the act of singing.
4. *Kridali* — the act of playing, especially indigenous games like *narikel karakari* (snatching the coconut).[8]
5. *Mallali* — a kind of wrestling (essential for both body-building and self-defence).
6. *Birali* — cultivating noble acts, including courage, chivalry towards women and respect for the elderly.
7. *Sevali* — the act of caring for people, animals and plants.
8. *Shilpali* — arts and crafts, including painting, and sewing and embroidery.
9. *Gyanali* — the act of cultivating knowledge.
10. *Chashali* — the act of agricultural cultivation.
11. *Dakhhtali* — the act of specialization or expertise in any of the varieties of acts: horse-riding, boating, writing books etc.

12. *Sandyanali* — the act of meditation.
13. *Faujali* — cultivating a sense of military discipline and control.
14. *Kathali* — the act of articulate speaking.
15. *Bhramantali* — the act of travelling as a way of learning.
16. *Koutukali* — the act of humour, reflecting Dutta's belief that Bengalis were missing 'joy' in their lives.[9]

As the vows, additional vows, promises, prohibitions and acts listed above illustrate, the movement was obviously meant to develop a better generation of Bengalis than those found at that time. The dream of developing a race that would be virile, masculine and embedded in its 'authentic' culture is manifested in these normative behaviours prescribed for the disciples of the Bratachari movement. The idea was to attain spiritual growth through disciplining the corporeal body. Rhythm played an important part here as recital of the vows, prohibitions and promises included rhythmic body movements.

The observance of various vows and acts was structured into a programme of daily activities into which he introduced a few "traditional" folk dances thought to have long been a part of Bengali village culture. He believed that each individual has a distinctive core that essentially differs from that of others. Similarly, he pointed out that each nation had inherent traits, or Soul Characteristics. These are reflected most prominently through emotional, rather than rational expressions.

Gurusaday Dutta's efforts at reviving the folk tradition were regarded with suspicion by the British government, which was generally wary of attempts at organizing people around physical culture following the prominence of *akharas* (gyms) in the seditious activities surrounding the Swadeshi movement. Despite his status as a district magistrate, the government engaged an officer to keep a close watch on him, who suspected Dutta of forming a group of bandits.[10] Despite these concerns, and those of local who considered his passion for folk song and dance as the whims of a mentally unsound man, Dutta was later recognized and acknowledged by James Buchanam, the Director of Physical Education curriculum to be followed in government schools. To train teacher and other enthusiasts, a folk dance training camp was first held in 1932 at Suri, the district headquarters of Birbhum district when he was posted as district officer. Bratachari movement was the development of physical strength combined with an "inner rhythm". This was also the aim of a number of physical culture movement that grew up in colonial Bengal during this time; that also wanted to create a "Perfect man" who was physically vigorous, mentally agile and morally strong.

Gurusaday Dutta was keen to recover aspects of Bengali culture that had been eclipsed by the growth of English Education. Indeed, he saw 'tradition' our encapsulating and masculine essence of Bengal. He wished to see Bengali men being recruited into any cadre serving the nation. In his biography of his wife, written by him, he recalled that Saroj Nalini Dutta formed women's organizations that used to knit for the Bengali soldier in the army and that she felicitated the soldiers when they visited the districts where he was posted.[11]

Dutta was known for his fierce admiration of Indian, especially Bengali traditions. Indeed, he considered them to be far better than those of the Western world, and therefore, firmly believed that India had the potential to show the rest of the world the real meaning of progress. He did not hide his displeasure at mechanized and urbanized Western culture and mourned the fact that Bengali youth, especially the English-educated middle class, tended to imitate Western ideas while ignoring the traditions of their own country; indeed, he maintained that this was the cause of the deterioration of the race.[12] As a result, he repeated over and over the importance of reviving 'tradition' in order to resurrect the nation. There was a deep nostalgia in Dutta's writings which led him to instruct readers that in order to regain the joy that had once existed in Bengali society, one needed to become a *bratachari*.

In 1928-29, when Gurusaday Dutta, an officer in the Indian Civil Service, visited England and was present at a festival organized by the English Folk Dance Society, and was impressed by the demonstration of British 'folk elements' at the festival. This event proved to be quite an eye-opener for Dutta, who appropriated the idea of the authenticity of folk cultures on his return to India, becoming an avid collector of 'indigenous' folk arts. From 1929 to 1940, he collected from various Bengali villages more than two thousand samples of various folk arts, including *pat*, *kanthas*, dolls, ornaments, earthen vessels and so on. He later wrote that he was glad to note the apparent similarity seen in the folk dances performed in England and those he remembered from his childhood.[13]

The folk traditions he had in minds, which were in need of revival, included *kirtan*, a form of emotional songs that apparently had been quite common in his childhood. *Kirtan* had since declined in popularity due to the development of what Dutta identified as a 'hybrid' culture among Bengali especially the English-educated urban middle class that had little regard for folk music.

The deployment of 'authentic' folk dances such as *raibneshe*, *kathi* and *Jan*, therefore, formed a central, yet problematic aspect of the movement. Dutta maintained the idea that a 'folk tradition' reflected the quintessential nature of a certain 'race'. He stated that in the pre-colonial period, and even during early colonial times, Bengalis had relied on these dance forms to keep themselves healthy. Indeed, he even argued that these dances were actually performed by warriors and thus contained martial qualities. But as Bengalis had become more 'modem' and engaged in the imperial project *via* education and employment, they had become detached from their 'martial' roots, instead mindlessly imitating European civilization. Dutt classified 'indigenous' dance forms as 'tokens of the spontaneous growth of the socio-religious life of a race and, therefore, far superior to those forms which are consciously cultivated by a culture or civilization'. He spoke about a 'loss of innocence' under the forceful thrust of an increasingly urbanized and industrialized society. His concern could be located in anxieties about 'frail' bodies and 'degenerate' moral fibre, and like many others in the Bengali middle class, he devolved the blame onto colonial rule. To demonstrate that Bengalis were indeed a 'martial race', he chose the *raibneshe* dance, which he essentially categorized as a war-dance traditionally practised by Bengalis, the residues of which could be found in 'virile' dances performed by lower caste men in some parts of Bengal. Curiously, at times, these dancers would dress up as women and perform semi-erotic dances, which Dutta maintained was symptomatic of the loss of taste on the part of the Bengali middle class. When it was pointed out to him that because they dressed like women, the dancers were called *raibneshe* (meaning dressed like Rai, or Radha, the consort of Lord Krishna), Dutta delegitimised that etymology, instead claiming a martial genealogy for the dance because the men, who held staves made of the best bamboo (*rai bnaash*), were called *raibneshe*.[14]

Gurusaday Dutta was also known for his interest and contributions to Bengal's folk art, folk dance, folk culture and music. He spend a life time collection and studying art objects and handwork from the remotest corners of undivided rural Bengal. Collecting items of folk art such as Kalighat paintings, patuas scrolls, embroidered kanthas, terracotta panels, stone sculptures, wooden carvings, doll and toys, moulds used for making patterns and sweets or mang-pasts etc. He established many originations for keeping folk culture. As like Mymensingh Folk Dance Folk Music Society (1929), Pallisampad Raksha Samiti (1931), Bratachari Lokanritya Samiti (1932), South India Bratachari Society (1932),

Sarbabharatiya Bratachari Society etc. In 1941, he also set up the Bratachari village near Calcutta and the Bratachari Janashiksha Pratishthan.

His fearless independence and indomitable spirit of nationalism brought him into conflict with the British Government on more than one occasion. In 1928, at Howrah, in connection with the Bamangachi Firing case, he condemned the firing on a crowd to protesters by the police led by a British officer. The matter was raised in the British House of Lords and Secretary of State of India in the British Government had to answer angry question. British parliamentarians wanted Dutta, referred to as this Indian officer, punished for having the audacity to question a British officer's action. As a punitive measure, he was transferred out of Howrah to Mymensingh. His stay in Mymensingh was also cut short when he failed to give orders as required by him by the British Indian Government to deal with protesters against the Salt Act had called for a Satyagraha against this Act. He was transferred to Birbhum by telegram, which was an unprecedented way of dealing with an ICS officer in those days. In his life he tried to prevent youth from the bad effect of Modern education and culture. He was not the anti of modernization. He obviously wanted youth can get modern scientific education but he also wanted that they cannot lose their own rhythm of culture and resources.

Conclusion

Bratachari Movement was based on the idea of revival of a golden part that seemed lost under colonial rule. In this case, revival implied the reorganization of specific "folk traditions" which marked as 'authentic'. Bratachari movement valued categories such as 'indigenous' and 'traditional'. The movement aimed at creating a sense of world citizenship as well as national awareness among people, irrespective of caste, religion, sex and age. The movement aimed to nature the mind and the body and to encourage people to work for national and individual improvement through encouraging traditional and folk culture, especially folk dance and song. The Bratachari follower pledged themselves to build their moral fibre and serve the country on the five principles of knowledge, labour, truth, unity and joy. They aimed at developing the mind and body through dance as well as by undertaking to perform good deeds.

NOTES

1. Dutta Gurusaday, *Bratachari Parichay*, Banglar Bratachari Samity, Calcutta, 1940, pp. 12-22.
2. Choudhuri Amit, *Gurusaday*, Banglar Bratachari Samiti, Calcutta, 1982, pp. 14-17.
3. Dutta Gurusaday, *The Bratachari Synthesis*, Banglar Bratachari Samiti, Calcutta, 1940, pp. 29-30.
4. *Knocha* is the lower end of a *dhoti*, the unstitched garment worn by Bengali men. Hanging the *knocha* not only signified luxury but also a sort of moral decadence and femininity.
5. He was disturbed by the practice of English-educated Bengalis speaking Bengali with a large number of English words thrown in; hence his emphasis on speaking an "Uncontaminated" forms of Bengali.
6. *Ibid.*, pp. 10-30.
7. *Ibid.*
8. Dutta Gurusaday, "Banglar Krishtidhara — Narikel Karakari: Banglar Samorik Krira", in Banglar Shakti, *Bhadro 1343*, Calcutta, 1st year, No. 2.
9. See Anonymous, "Bratachari Sholo Ali — Banglar Samorik Krira", in Banglar Shakti, *Jaishthyo 1345*, Calcutta, 2nd year, No. II.
10. Prasad De Sankar, *Swadashipremi Gurusaday*, Bratachari Kendriya Nayak Mandali, Calcutta, 1982, pp. 74-78.
11. Dutta Gurusaday (Rajiv Kundu, ed.), *Sarojnalini: Songkhipto Jibon*, Ababhas, Kolkata, 2014, pp. 92-95.
12. Dutta, *Bratachari Porichay*, pp. 21-26.
13. Dutta, *Introduction, Banglar Lokashilpa O Lokanrityo*, A Large part of his collection in new stored at the Gurusaday Dutta Museum, located at Joka, Kolkata, India.
14. Dutta Gurusaday, *The Folk Dance of Bengal*, Birendra Saday Dutta, Kolkata, 1945, see Introduction and Chapter 1.

11

History of Sanskrit Literature
Impact of Globalization Before and After

Biswajit Roy

Indian literature originated in the Vedic period. The Vedic prayers are a reflection of the simple life of that era. Later on, in the age of Upanishads, the feeling of a great power, the complex activities of the Brahmins, the picture of the management of the state and society in religion and memory can be seen. The images of mental transition are also captured in poetry and rhetoric but the existence of history is nowhere to be found.

The Sanskrit word '*Itihas*' is interpreted as '*Iti - Ha - As*'[1] or 'it was like this', i.e. a faithful account of what was happening then. Here can be any political, social, person-centred description, which will identify the features of the country-time-society of the era. But there no such specific evidence were found. For this, the reasons are as follows: (1) Indifference to the present life and interest in the hereafter. (2) Nomadism or impermanence in life from the age of Vedas. (3) Internal conflict and the constant attacks of foreign enemies. Nationalism did not awakened in India for these reasons and there was no tendency to preserve national history. The passage from one era to another through the chronology and chronology of history, the various features by their mutual comparison and above all the information of progress are found. India's highly advanced mindset is surprisingly silent about this.

Among them, researchers have traced the elements of history in Puranic literature specially from the *Ramayana* and the *Mahabharata*. '*Mahavamsa*' written by Mahanama in the fifth century A.D. and Pathabali of Jains. Very little real history has been found from it, excluding imagination and horrible exaggeration.

In later times script has been recognized as a true element of literary history. *Danapatra*, *prashasti* and other inscriptions are accurate relics of different eras. Surprisingly, later in the classical literary age, poems were written about special historical persons or dynasties but unfortunately, history is also neglected. This chapter discusses those essays. Sanskrit literature is full of literature, religion, philosophy, grammar, science and art. There is not only history in the vast tradition. We relate to the word "history" from the different past. In that ancient period, i.e. in the Vedic age, "Itihas — puranam panchamang bedananang bedam" (7/2). The *Mahabharata* mentions, "Itihas — Puranabhanga bedang samupabrang hainye". The economist Kautilya calls history the fifth Veda. In ancient India, the word history was synonymous with myths, legends, histories, theology etc. The word history of the ancient is the term modern history or English 'History' not synonymous to ancient events or stories, folktales, legends, anecdotes. Everything has become history. That very history of ancient India has not always spoken the truth.

Imagination is mixed with imagination and reality is lost. From the point of view of History, all those events can never get the dignity of history although the authors of the *Ramayana* and the *Mahabharata* call their poems history but none of them are history. Many historians consider the main events of the *Ramayana* and the *Mahabharata* as historical narratives. These two holy books are in fact mixed literary works.

There is a lot of information about the early stages in the history of India in the ancient and medieval times. Puranic dynasties, inscriptions, copperplates, Jains Pathabali[2] etc. have historical evidence. Besides these, as well as a number of prose poems, lyric poems, *champukabyas*, visuals and books also based on historical events. Although there are many historical events, they are not always accurate history. In the early days of the kings, almost all the kings were gracious poets. These poets used to compose poems of different tastes from time to time. These poets used to compose poems by praising the kings and ignoring the fact because they used to take food and water from the kings. Among those poems there was poetic imagination, extra words etc. but there was also a lot of poetry based on history. In ancient India, historians have found historical information from *Samudruagupta Prashasti* of Harishen, Ashoka's inscription, Aihole inscription, coins, testimonials, thousand years of rocky evidence etc. Foreign tourists have also given us a picture of history through their travel stories. All those beloved tourists are Megasthenes, Hiuen Tsang, Fa Hien, Al-Biruni and others.

India is a country of spirituality. Yet many historians have remained silent on the subject. Why no historical poetry of any of the best historians has been created in this country? Surprisingly, great poets like Balmiki — Beas, playwrites like Bhas — Kalidas — Bhavabhuti, writers like Dandin — Subandhu — Bana, storytellers like Bishnu Sharma — Narayan Sharma — Gunadhya philosophers like Kapil — Kanad — Goutam, Bharat — Bhamaha — Dandin — Anandabardhana — Jagannath like rhetorical, Aryabhatta — Varahmihir — Bhaskaracharya like astronomist, Charak — Jibak — Sushruta like physician and Panini — Katyayan — Patanjali[3] like auspicious grammarian were born in the holy land. Not a single person was born in the country who would make the slightest effort to capture the history of India. Regrettably, Dr. A.B. Keith says, "In the whole of the great period of Sanskrit literature, there is not one writer who can be seriously regarded as a critical historian."[4]

Indian poets with the plight as well as history of India there is no specific information about it. Many people say, "History is the one weak point in Sanskrit literature."[5] What is the reason for the obstruction of Indian historiography? Many have done research on this subject. Some of their important views are discussed below:

First of all, the political environment in India was not conducive from a few centuries before the birth of Christ to about the twelfth century A.D. Foreign powers have repeatedly attacked India. Every time India has lost. No attempt has been made in India in the past to record the history of defeat. Mr. Keith rightly said: "It may be that India failed to produce historians because the great political event which affected her during the period up to A.D. 1200 did not call forth popular action. . . ."[6]

Secondly, the negative attitude of Indian philosophers towards real life has become an obstacle to historiography. The sages of India have said: 'Brahma Satyanjajanmithya', 'Tyagachanti Nirantaram', 'Ten Tyakten Bhungitha', 'Koupinbanta: Khalu Bhagyabanta'.[7] They have spent their life by trying to assimilate the words of Advaita Vedanta. What is the time to look at real history?

Thirdly, a nation's history is inspired by its own sense of nationalism. But it goes without saying that a sense of nationalism has not emerged in fragmented India.

Fourthly, it goes without saying that, the two ancient scriptures of India, the *Ramayana* and the *Mahabharata* did not try to preserve history. However, the old literature has tried to preserve history.

Dynasties and genealogical descriptions are among the five signs of the Puranas.[8]

In spite of these adversities, it cannot be said that, there was no attempt to preserve history in ancient India. It cannot be said that, Sanskrit history was unconscious. Banabhatta's *Harshacharita* prose poetry contains various informations about emperor Harshavardhana. Parimal's *Nabasahasanka*, Bihlanera's *Bikramankadeba*, Hemchandra's *Kumarapalacharita*, Sandhyakara Nandi's *Ramacharita*, Jayanakera's *Prthbirajabijaya*, Bakpatirajera's *Gaurabadha*, Nayachandra Suri's *Hammirakavya*, Chandrasekhar's *Surjanacharita*, Rudrakabir's *Rastraurhabansakabya*, Rajnath Dindimera's *Achyutarabhyudaya*, Dhoyi's *Pavanduta*, Kabisambhura's *Rajendrakarnapura*, Jairam Pandey's *Radhamadhav Bilaschampu*, Kesabpanditera's *Rajaramacharita* included the name of the memorable, Kalhan's *Raj Tarangini*[9] is undoubtedly the best composition of this genre.

Banabhatta's *Harshacharita Akhyayika* class of prose poetry written in the background of history. There is no doubt, Harshavardhana's poetry will be helpful in gaining knowledge about history during the reign of Maharaja Harshavardhana and his reign. History can also the gleaned from various inscriptions and accounts of Hiuen Tsang. There are many similarities between the historical information of Hiuen Tsang and the *Harshacharita* of Banabhatta. Banabhatta had little interest in narrating the history of the Sthanbishwar Dynasty because he is a poet not a historian. He could not get of the coveted poetic path. Needles to say, the appeal of the poem would have multiplied a thousand fold if the *Harshacharita* had been composed from a historical point of view. Historical romance of the poet Bana's, i.e. there are eight exuberances in the *Harshacharita* known as *Ramayana*. The poet has also narrated the story of the poem by describing the identity of his family. Puspabhuti was the king of Sthanbishwar. Prabhakarabardhana was born in that dynasty. Prabhakarabardhana tied the knot with Ujjainiraj Yashovardhan Vikramaditya's daughter Yashomati. Prabhakarabardhana defeated the Huns. The kings of Gurjar, Indus, Gandhara, Lat and Malabdesh were also defeated by him. Prabhakarabardhana had two sons. Their names were Rajyavardhana and Harshavardhana. His daughter's name was Rajyashree. Ujjainiraj Shiladitya acknowledged the dominance of Prabhakara. Kumargupta and Malabgupta were two sons of one Malabraj. Both were befriended. Prabhakarabardhana's sons lived in Rajbari. Sadly, the poet did not say the name of Malabraj, but 'one', saying the name would have filled the historical document. Rajyashree was married to Grahavarman, the eldest son of Maukhariraja Avantivarman. The capital of the Grahavarman was Kanyakubja or Kannauj. At the young age Rajyavardhana fought with the Feudal Lords against the Huns. On the day of Prabhakar's death, Grahavarman was killed by Malavaraj and Rajyashree was imprisoned. As soon as this news was heard, Rajyavardhana was setup to fight against Malavaraj. Rajyavardhana was killed in the conspiracy of Gauraja. In such a situation, Harshavardhana declared war with Skandhagupta and freed Rajyashree. The story is very short. The poet was only eager to describe the joys and sorrows of Harsha's lile, victory and defeat etc. He has included various non-historical issues in his poetry. He has remained silent while presenting the information of history. Although the poet mentioned Harsha's month and date of birth, he did not mention the year. Gaurraj mentioned one of the assassins of Rajyavardhana but did not introduce himself. The clash of Rajyavardhana with the Huns started. As a result, the battle of Rajyavardhana and Malvaraja began, the betrayal of Gauraj and punishment by Harsh. The poet has remained silent about the details of Gaurraj's suppression. There is a lot information available about Harshavardhana from Guptalek. But no information was found from Bana's poetry. However, it has to be admitted that, Banabhatta has tried to give some historical information. In the History of Sanskrit literature by Dasgupta and De says, "The sum — total of the story, Lavishly embellished as it is, is no more than an incident of Harsha's carrier; and it cannot be said that the picture is either full or satisfactory from the historical point of view."

The historical poem composed by Padmagupta was written in 1005 A.D. The poem is more fictional than historical. Padmagupta's father's name was Mrigankagupta. Padmagupta was the court poet of the virtuous king Munj of the Parmar dynasty of Dhara city. Munj's other name was Nabasahsanka. Munja's title was Bakpatiraj. Padmagupta praised Satavahana, Vikramaditya and Sriharsha in his poetry. The main theme of the poem is the love and marriage of Sindhuraja and Nagrajkumari Shashiprabha. The material of the actual history formed in the structure of the mythological story is quite insignificant. The poem is Sindhuraja of Malab gives a slight indication of the historical facts of the Nabasahsanka. Padmagupta is a talented poet. He has satisfied with composing history based poems due to his disinterest in history writing.

Vikramank Dev Charita was written by the Kashmiri poet Bilhan. It has written the history of the Chalukya Dynasty kings in 18 sermons.

The poem is about wars and marriages of the dynasty. In the eleventh century, Bilhan arrived at Kalyanpur the capital of Tribhuvan-Malla Bikramankadev.[10] The Chalukya king rewarded the poet with Chhatra and Gaj and conferred the title of Vidyapati. The conflict started between Vikramaditya and Jayasingha over the right to the throne. The defeat of the Chola King by the middle son Vikramaditya and the establishment of his own dominion. The suppression of Jayasingha by Vikramaditya and established Vikrampur. He constructed the temple of Vishnu and the Kanchi kingdom. The text of all the inscriptions found at that time has been recovered and the alleged Chalukya of Bilhan has been found. There is not much discrepancy in that history with the dynasty. The background of Sanskrit epic writers composing epic poems is the highest. The value of history has been diminished even though the humour of poetry has made the book brighter than the clear view of history in the work of the poet. Poems, plays or champu or lyric poems written by Jainacharyas based on historical stories have very little historical value. The only exception among the epics is Hemchandra's *Kumarapalacharita*. This epic is written in two languages. There are a total of 28 cantos in the poem. The first 20 cantos are in Sanskrit and the next 8 cantos are in Prakrit language. The author describes the history of the Chalukya Dynasty Anhilism. The story of Kumarapala's ancestors, namely Mulraj, Chamundraya, Ballavraja, Dullavaraja, Bhima, Karna and Jaisingh is also narrated in the book. Although the poem contains historical information, the ideological propaganda of Jainism has prevailed over the poetic quality. Hemchandra gained a great reputation as a preacher of Jainism from 1089-1173 A.D. Needless to say, the book failed to garner praise for not having a detailed account of history.

In the twelfth century AD, the Bengali poet Sandhyakara Nandi composed the historical poem 'Ramacharit'. In four chapters, the poct narrates in 220 verses in Aryachhanda the deeds of Ramachandra, the hero of *Ramayana*, and Rampal, the king of the Pala Dynasty, and his successor. It is known from the poet's praise that the poet's father's name is Prajapati Nandi and his grandfather's name is Pinakandi. He was a Kayastha or Karan in the nation. Sandhyakara's father was a peace treaty of Rampal, a king of the Pala Dynasty. The poet calls his poem "Clical Balmiki." The story of *Ramayana* was secondary. The period of Rampal is from 1064-1130 A.D. Along with describing Rampal's character, he also wrote biographies of Kumar Pal, Tritiya Gopal and Madan Pal. This poem is the last poem from the point of view of rhetoricians. Historiography has become trivial in poetry as more attention has been paid to royalty.

Kashmiri poet Jayanayak wrote a historical poem called "Prithviraj Vijay." The book is incomplete. It has 12 cantos. The story of the ancestors of the last Hindu King Prithviraj of the Middle Ages and even his marriage is narrated. The first serge of the poem tells the story of the origin of Chahuman, i.e. Chauhan Dynastry.

The second serge deals with the Chauhan kings and the Mlechha king with the responsibility of killing. The third canto contains descriptions of the Chauhan Dynasty. The last 4 sermons tell the life story of Prithviraj. The author has narrated the story of Prithviraj's pre-birth, the story of his coronation, the story of conjugal life, the conquest campaign etc. in detail. But, the story of his conflict with Mohammed Ghori has been narrated very briefly. The value of Prithviraj's conquest as a historical poem is insignificant. Jayanayak probably wrote the book in the twelfth century.

In "Hammirkavya" Nayachandra Suri describes the biographies of the Chauhan Dynastry kings in 1582 verses in 14 cantos in the 1500s. The poet narrates the biographies of a total of 26 famous Rajput kings of medieval history. Among the kings, Prithviraj and Hampi are particularly notable.

Rabindra Paramananda Khishti wrote "Shivabharat Kavya" about the life of Shivaji in the 1800s. The poem describes Shivaji's war with the Mughals and the defeat of the Mughals from his childhood in 32 cantos.

This historical encyclopaedia was written in the twelfth century by Dhoyi, the poet of Lakshman Sen. In his poem, Lakshman Sen is portrayed as a monster.

> Dantibyuhang konkalatikang chamarang haimdantang
> Yo gourendradalvat kavikakshmabhutang chakravarti.
> Sridhoyik Saklarasikaprithetormanasvi
> Kabyang sarasvatamib mahamantrametajjagad.[11]

Kalhana's *Raj Tarangini* is one of the best historical works in Sanskrit literature. Kalhana himself received the patronage of Raja Jayasingha and Alokdatta. The poem *Raj Tarangini* was composed in the twelfth century. It seems that he left the ministry and concentrated on the study of history. He always studied poetry. He was well acquainted with the poems of *Ramayana*, *Mahabharata*, *Raghuvamsa*, *Harshacharita*,

Bilhan, Mankha etc. He became a novice in composing poetry by constantly studying ancient legends, copperplates, inscriptions, *Nilmat Purana*, Kshemendra's *Nripavali*, ancient mythology etc. In his books we have been able to get a perfect knowledge of Kashmir dynasty information, contemporary history, geography, sociology, politics etc. The historical description of the ancient Indian tradition given by the poet is in one word impeccable. *Raj Tarangini* has become a complete history due to the combination of the poet's insight and the historian's ever-awakening real consciousness. The history of Kashmir at the time of Kalhan was complicated by internal war fare and politics. When Harsha ascended the throne, peace was maintained for some time. When Harsha was killed by the Damaras, the fire of unrest flared up again. In his poem, he has highlighted the various practices of each community of the society of that time. In his poem, the poet raises the issue of mutual revenge of the power-hungry kings, domination of the economy etc. Kalhan describes the geographical location of all the rivers, cities, temples, monasteries and ancient pilgrimage sites in Kashmir. *Raj Tarangini* is indispensable poem it comes to mapping ancient Kashmir.

The words 'historical poetry' arise controversy. The present poem is the poet's imagination. According to Biswanath, 'Bakyangrasatmakang kavyam' means humorous sentence in poetry. History is a fact that happened in ancient times. In the one hand poetry, on the other hand history, the poets have bound these two opposing entities in a web of imagination. Some imagination, some reality, has been created in a mixture of these two. Historical poetry and the reader's interest has been existed there for a long time.

The aversion to the history of India came mainly from the aversion of this world. Internal instability, disunity etc. have also been cited as ancillary causes. But thc globalization of India has not stopped for all this. Analyzing the word 'globalization', we find two words *Viswa* (Earth) + *Ioan* (Motion), meaning 'going to the world or spreading to the world'. Could self-centred India became known to the world ? Did that feature spread to the wider field ? The reflection of globalization can be found in the answers of these questions.

India is a very prosperous country. In ancient times, there was unclear idea about it. Alexander's invasion in the 300 Century BC left a trial of foreigners on the country's soil. It was during this time when a Greek tourist named Megasthenes came to this country and write his travelogue about the prosperity of this country to curiosity about.

Then the Mauryan Emperor Ashoka preached the message of Lord Buddha in many countries. Since then, a deep connection has been established between China and India for the propagation of Buddhism. In his travel stories, he wrote about various Buddhist pilgrimage centres, books and social system for the same purpose.

From the tenth century in the middle ages, Al Beruni (1024-1030 A.D.), Marco Polo of Italy (1288-1292 A.D.), Ibn Battuta of Morocco (1333-1347 A.D.), Abdur Razzak of Iran (1443-1444 A.D.), Tadarniyer from French (1605-1689 A.D.), such well known tourists came to India. Through them, the knowledge of India spread all over the world. *Aryabhata*, an Indian mathematician became famous in the Middle East and Greece after being translated his books. In addition with like *Panchatantra* etc. were also translated into Pahlavi and reached different parts of the w0rld. On the other hand, Buddhist scriptures were taken across Tibet to Mongolia, China and other places. Ayurveda in India also occupies a very prestigious position in East and Central Asia. In this way, the knowledge of India became the title of the whole world. On the other hand, various merchant classes of India introduced spices, silk, cotton and cotton clothes and many other materials to the world. In this way, India became Globalized.

NOTES

1. Dhirendranath Bandyopadhyaya, *Sanskrita Sahityer Itihas*, West Bengal State Book Board, September 2015/e, p. 427.
2. A.D. Pusalkar, "Conception of History in Ancient Indian Literature", *OH*, Vol. XII, Pt. II, pp. 35-ff.
3. Yudhisthir Gop, *History of Sanskrit Literature*, Sanskrit Book Depot, Reprint, September 2010, p. 238.
4. *A History of Sanskrit Literature*, A.B. Keith.
5. Yudhisthir Gop, *History of Sanskrit Literature*, Sanskrit Book Depot, Reprint, September 2010, p. 238.
6. *A History of Sanskrit Literature*, A.B. Keith.
7. Yudhisthir Gop, *History of Sanskrit Literature*, Sanskrit Book Depot, Reprint, September 2010, p. 238.
8. Yudhisthir Gop, *History of Sanskrit Literature*, Sanskrit Book Depot, Reprint, September 2010, p. 239.
9. Dhirendranath Bandyopadhyaya, *Sanskrita Sahityer Itihas*, West Bengal State Book Board, September 2015/e, p. 428.
10. Yudhisthir Gop, *History of Sanskrit Literature*, Sanskrit Book Depot, Reprint, September 2010, p. 242.
11. Chakraborty Chintaharan, "Pavandutam", Sanskrit Sahitya Parishad.

REFERENCES

Bandyopadhyay Dhirendranath, *History of Sanskrit Literature*, West Bengal State Book Board, *Ashar* 1395.

Chakraborty Chintaharan, *Pavandutam*, Sanskrit Sahitya Parishad.

Dasgupta, S.N., University of Calcutta, 1975.

Gop Yudhisthira's, *History of Sanskrit Literature*, Sanskrit Book Depot, Reprint September 2010.

Section – III

Political Aspects of Globalization

12

Socio-Economic and Political Upliftment of the Dalits
Globalization and After

Krishna Kanta Dhali

Introduction

Traditionally the so-called Untouchables or *Dalits* were seen as un-clean in a religious sense and presumed to defile others by their touch or presence. It is understood that they had to live in separate areas, at some distance from others. It is retrieved that they were born for the purpose of serving others, it was believed that they carried out the occupations dealing with ritually defiled materials. According to historical reference, *Dalit* movement was going on since ancient time and it is running till now. In the 19th century, Gopal Baba Walangkar (c. 1840-1900) is generally considered to be the pioneer of the *Dalit* movement, seeking a society in which they were not discriminated against. Another pioneer was Harichand Thakur (1812-1878) with his Matua organization that involved the Namasudra (Chandal) community in the Bengal Presidency. Ambedkar himself believed Walangkar to be the progenitor. Another early social reformer who worked to improve conditions of *Dalits* was Jyotirao Phule (1827-1890). Providing elementary education, basic health services and ensuring nutritious food to *Dalits* has become far-away dream. In this sense, education and other all kinds of reading and writing was not for those who lack a *Varna*, the scriptures stated in India.[1]

Socio-economic and Political Conditions

Modern thought, literature, institutions, modern research and the impact of globalization have changed the mental thinking of man to develop the socio-economic and political conditions. *Dalit* communities are also going on to change themselves in the world including the Indian society. For this purpose the 'National Campaign on Dalit Human Rights (NCDHR)' was formed in the year 1998. 'Let Us Cast Out Caste' is the first folder published by the 'National Campaign on Dalit Human Rights (NCDHR)'. Under the faces, the folder's front page text is repeated: "Dalits. A People. A Culture. A History." Another addition is "We Demand Freedom From Caste Bondage For 260 Million Dalits Of Asia."[2] These black bold letters are to make them materialistic, memorable and associated with the campaign and they seem to work as a logo. It is the small thought of Ambedkar. The themes are a good example of how the NCDHR wants to put *Dalits* into the Global discourse on human rights. Its fact that first and foremost *Dalits* are projected to an international audience with associations with Aboriginals or indigenous people in other parts of the world. Globalization is playing a pivotal role in shaping the future India in terms of economy, agriculture, social, political conditions of *Dalits*. It has integrated rich, affluent, and educated classes, but has fractured working classes of marginalized sections such as *Dalit*, who do not have the skills and economic clout to profit from open markets. Hundreds of millions of *Dalits* across the country, the actual effects of neo-liberal policies have been inequality, poverty, hunger, increased susceptibility to disease and sickness, and economic and political marginalization.

Social Conditions and *Dalit* Literatures

The 1950 Constitution of India, introduced after the country gained independence included measures to improve the socio-economic conditions of *Dalits*. Aside from banning untouchability, these included the reservation system, a means of positive discrimination that created the classifications of Scheduled Castes, Scheduled Tribes for *Dalits*. Communities that were categorized as being one of those groups were guaranteed a percentage of the seats in the national and state legislatures, as well as in government jobs and places of education. The system has its origins in the 1932 Poona Pact between Ambedkar and Gandhi, when Ambedkar conceded his demand that the *Dalits* should have an electorate separate from the caste Hindus in return for Gandhi accepting measures along these lines. The notion of a separate electorate had been proposed in the Communal Award made by the British Raj authorities and the outcome of the Pact, the Government of India Act of 1935 — both introduced the new term of *Scheduled Castes* in replacement for *Depressed Classes* and reserved seats for them in the legislatures.

Dalit literature forms a distinct part of Indian literature. One of the first *Dalit* writers was Madara Chennaiah, an eleventh-century cobbler-saint who lived in the reign of West Chalukyas and who is regarded by some scholars as the "father of Vachana poetry." Another early *Dalit* poet is Dohara Kakkaiah, a *Dalit* by birth, six of whose confessional poems survive. The Bharatiya Dalit Sahitya Akademi (Indian Dalit Literature Academy) was founded in 1984 by Babu Jagjivan Ram. Notable modern authors include Mahatma Phule and Ambedkar in Maharashtra, who focused on the issues of *Dalits* through their works and writings. This started a new trend in *Dalit* writing and inspired many *Dalits* to offer work in Marathi, Hindi, Tamil and Punjabi. There are novels, poems and even drama on *Dalit* issues. The Indian author Rajesh Talwar has written a play titled 'Gandhi, Ambedkar, and the Four Legged Scorpion' in which the personal experiences of Dr. Ambedkar and the sufferings of the community have been highlighted. In 19th century, many *Dalit* literatures are found in Bengal like '*Sri Sri Hari Lilamrito*' written by Tarak Chandra Sarkar, '*Sri Sri Hari Guruchand Charitro Sudha*' written by Tarak Chandra Sarkar, '*Guruchand Charit*' written by Mahananda Halder. All are the primary books for the *Dalit* Namasudra literatures in Bengal. The literacy rate of total population in West Bengal is 68.6 per cent, which further dwindles to 63.4 per cent for total rural population. On the contrary, the literacy among total *Dalits* is only 59.04 per cent, which further reduces to 48.91 per cent among rural *Dalits*. Hence, in terms of educational attainment, the urban population is found to be advanced. Similarly, the educational attainment of *Dalit* is far more modest than the State average. Again, if gender disparity is imputed in educational attainment, the variation of male-female literacy rate of total population is 17.4 per cent against the corresponding disparity of *Dalit* population whooping 23.63 per cent. Among the *Dalits*, Sunri (excluding Saha) with 82.5 per cent literacy is on top of the list.[3] Other *Dalits* who have recorded literacy rate higher than the state average are Dhoba 73.9 per cent, Pod or Paundra (72.1%), Namasudra (71.9%), Jalia Kaibartta (64.9%), Tiyar (62.1%), and Rajbangshi (69%). Bauri have the lowest literacy rate 37.5 per cent. The gender gap in literacy is highest among Lohar and Bauri (29 percentage points), and it is comparatively small 16 per cent among Namasudra and Jhalo Malo. So, in terms of educational attainment, progress of Sunri, Dhoba, Pod or Paundra and Namasudra are relatively better.[4] In the second half of 1980s *Dalit* women came to express a need for a separate platform within the wider women's struggle, for increasing their power in society. About 200 women from the south of India, Delhi, Maharashtra, Uttar Pradesh and West Bengal are said to have attended in the first Dalit Women's National Meeting for Dalit Women's Struggle and Aspirations in 1987. This was the beginning of a national network of Dalit Women which on 11 August, 1995 formed the NFDW.

Economic Condition

By 1995, of all federal government jobs in India — 10.1 per cent of Class I, 12.7 per cent of Class II, 16.2 per cent of Class III, and 27.2 per cent of Class IV jobs were held by *Dalits*.[5] Of the most senior jobs in government agencies and government-controlled enterprises, only 1 per cent were held by *Dalits*, not much change in 40 years. In the 21st century, Meira Kumar and Kumari Mayawati as the *Dalit* leaders have been elected to India's highest judicial and political offices.[6] In 2001, the quality of life of the *Dalit* population in India was worse than that of the overall Indian population on metrics such as access to health care, life expectancy, education attainability, access to drinking water and housing.[7] According to a 2014 report of the Ministry of Minority Affairs over 44.8 per cent of Scheduled Tribe (ST) and 33.8 per cent of Scheduled Caste (SC) populations in rural India were living below the poverty line. In 2011-12, in urban areas, 27.3 per cent of ST and 21.8 per cent of SC populations were below the poverty line.[8] NCDHR supported a study that gathered statistics from 11 states and over 565 villages throughout India. A sampling of these statistics is provided below to emphasize the violence and discrimination that occurs against *Dalits* on a daily basis. Up to 38 per cent of *Dalit* children in government schools are forced to sit separately while eating, in 20 per cent of schools, *Dalit* children are not allowed to drink from thc same water source, 27.6 per cent of *Dalits* are not permitted to enter police stations, 25.7 per cent have been denied access to ration shops, 33 per cent of public health workers have refused to visit *Dalit* homes, 48.4 per cent of *Dalits* in villages have been denied access to the public water source, 73 per cent *Dalits* have not been allowed to enter a non-*Dalit* home, 70 per cent have been denied eating with non-*Dalits*, in 10-20 per cent of villages surveyed *Dalits* were not allowed to wear "clean, bright or fashionable clothing."[9] Some *Dalits* have achieved affluence, although most remain poor. Some *Dalit* intellectuals, such as Chandra Bhan Prasad, have argued that the living standards of many *Dalits* have improved since the economic system became more liberalized starting in 1991 and have supported their claims through large surveys.[10] According to the Census 2011, nearly 79 per cent of *Adivasi* households and 73 per cent of *Dalit* households were the most deprived among rural households in India. While 45 per cent of SC households are landless and earn a living by manual casual labour, the figure is 30 per cent for *Adivasis*.[11] In West Bengal, among the *Dalit* landholdings, 80.97 per cent is marginal, 13.61 per cent is small, and only 0.01 per cent is large. A 2012 survey by Mangalore University in Karnataka found that 93 per cent of *Dalit* families in the state of Karnataka live below the poverty line.[12] In West Bengal the percentage of *Dalit* workers to total population (WPR) is only 38.8 per cent, which is lower than the aggregated figure for *Dalit* at the national level (i.e. 40.4%) but slightly above than total population in the State (i.e. 36.77%). Of the total *Dalit* workers, 74 per cent are recorded as main workers and 26 per cent as marginal workers. The female WPR is 22.31 per cent only, which is quite low when compared with male (i.e. 54.37%). The overwhelming workers among males are main workers (84.8%), while the ratio of main and marginal workers among female is evenly poised.[13] According to a 2007 report by Human Rights Watch (HRW), the treatment of *Dalits* has been like a "hidden apartheid" and that they "endure segregation in housing, schools, and access to public services."[14] The obvious similarities, race prejudice and the situation of *Dalits* "have a different basis and perhaps a different solution."[15] Though the Constitution of India abolished untouchability, the oppressed status of *Dalits* remains a reality. In rural India, "they still live in secluded quarters, do the dirtiest work, and are not allowed to use the village well and other common facilities."[16] In spite of much progress over the last sixty years, *Dalits* are still at the social and economic bottom of society.[17] While discrimination against *Dalits* has declined in urban areas and in the public sphere, it still exists in rural areas and in the private sphere, in everyday matters such as access to eating places, schools, temples and water sources. Some *Dalits* successfully integrated into urban Indian society, where caste origins are less obvious. In rural India, however, caste origins are more readily apparent and *Dalits* often remain excluded from local religious life, though some qualitative evidence suggests that exclusion is diminishing.[18]

According to the 2014 NCAER/University of Maryland survey, 27 per cent of the Indian population still practices untouchability; the figure may be higher because many people refuse to acknowledge doing so when questioned. Across India, untouchability was practised among

52 per cent of Brahmins, 33 per cent of Other Backward Classes and 24 per cent of non-Brahmin forward castes.[19] Untouchability was also practiced by people of minority religions — 23 per cent of Sikhs, 18 per cent of Muslims and 5 per cent of Christians. According to statewide data, Untouchability is most commonly practiced in Madhya Pradesh 53 per cent, followed by Himachal Pradesh 50 per cent, Chhattisgarh 48 per cent, Rajasthan and Bihar 47 per cent, Uttar Pradesh 43 per cent, and Uttarakhand 40 per cent.[20] According to 2011 Census, statewide SC people are 23.51 per cent in West Bengal, Tamil Nadu 20.01 per cent, Himachal Pradesh 25.19 per cent, Madhya Pradesh 15.62 per cent, Uttar Pradesh 20.70 per cent.[21] *Dalit* people are in huge number but economically, socially and politically they are in shortage. According to an analysis by the IndiaGoverns Research Institute, *Dalits* constituted nearly half of primary school dropouts in Karnataka during the period 2012-2014. After 2014, Government strategy have changed. A sample survey in 2014 conducted by "Dalit Adhikar Abhiyan" and funded by Action Aid found that among state schools in Madhya Pradesh, 88 per cent discriminated against *Dalit* children. In 79 per cent of the schools studied, *Dalit* children are forbidden from touching mid-day meals. They are required to sit separately at lunch in 35 per cent schools, and are required to eat with specially marked plates in 28 per cent.[22] There have been incidents and allegations of SC and ST teachers and professors being discriminated against and harassed by authorities, upper caste colleagues and upper caste students in different education institutes of India.[23] Such harassment cases are not demolished till now. After independence of 76 years, *Dalits* and poor people have not been getting their respect in Indian society. In some cases, such as in Gujarat, state governments have argued that, far from being discriminatory, their rejection when applying for jobs in education has been because there are no suitable qualified candidate from those classifications. Discrimination can also exist in access to healthcare and nutrition. A sample survey of *Dalits*, conducted over several months in Madhya Pradesh and funded by Action Aid in 2014, found that health field workers did not visit 65 per cent of *Dalit* settlements. 47 per cent of *Dalits* were not allowed entry into ration shops; and 64 per cent were given less grains than non-*Dalits*.[24] In Haryana state, 49 per cent of *Dalit* children under five years were underweight and malnourished while 80 per cent of those in the 6-59 months age group were anaemic in 2015.[25] According to following report, it is clear that *Dalit* people are not getting proper facilities to improve their socio-economic and political situation. But they should try to progress there in every field.

Political Conditions

Several *Dalit* groups are rivals and sometimes communal tensions are evident. We know more than 900 *Dalit* sub-castes throughout India, with internal divisions. Emphasizing any one caste threatens what is claimed to be an emerging *Dalit* identity and fostering rivalry among SCs. One thing is clear that it is easier to organize *Dalits* on a caste basis than to fight caste prejudice itself. It may be said with an example that Balmikis and Pasis in the 1990s refused to support the BSP, claiming it was a Jatav party but over 80 per cent of *Dalits* from all united *Dalit* castes voted BSP to power in 2007. The impacts of socio-cultural globalization have certainly played an important role in consolidating the BSP in UP and all over India. It would be safe to surmise that many of the SC candidates play a leading role in the SC politics of their respective constituencies all over India. For example, the BSP's progress in Lok Sabha Elections in UP is like the following. BSP increased its votes in 1985 by percentage of votes — 2.6 per cent, in 1989 votes percentage — 9.5 per cent, in 1991 percentage of votes — 11.9 per cent, in 1996 votes percentage — 20.6 per cent and in 1998 votes percentage — 22 per cent.[26] In West Bengal, the political condition of *Dalits* was not better. After Independence, Indian National Congress ruled here but *Dalit* representatives were not there without Pramatha Ranjan Thakur. Many converted *Dalit* Sikhs claim a superior status over the Hindu Raigars, Joatia, Chamars and Ravidasis and sometimes refuse to intermarry with them. They are divided into *Gotras* that regulate their marriage alliances. In Andhra Pradesh, Mala and Madiga were constantly in conflict with each other but as of 2015 Mala and Madiga students work for common *Dalit* cause at University level. Although the Khateek (butchers) are generally viewed as a higher caste than Bhangis, the latter refuse to offer cleaning services to Khateeks, believing that their profession renders them unclean. They also consider the Balai, Dholi and Mogya as unclean and do not associate with them.

In modern times, various political parties have been formed but Bahujan Samaj Party is one of the most popular and effective Indian Dalit party. This party is going on war against social, economical, political injustice to the *Dalits*. Other *Dalit* political parties are Republican Party of India active in Maharashtra; Viduthalai Chiruthaigal Katchi and Puthiya Tamilagam are the two major *Dalit* parties in Tamil Nadu; Bharipa Bahujan Mahasangh led by Prakash Yashwant Ambedkar, the grandson of Ambedkar; Lok Janasakti Party in Bihar. Anti-*Dalit* prejudices exist in groups such as the extremist militia Ranvir Sena largely run by upper-caste landlords in Bihar. They oppose equal treatment of *Dalits* and have resorted to violence. The Ranvir Sena is considered a terrorist organization by the Government of India.[27] The rise of *Hindutva's* (Hindu nationalism) role in Indian politics has accompanied allegations that religious conversions of *Dalits* are due to allurements like education and jobs rather than faith. Critics argue that laws banning conversion and limiting social relief for converts mean that conversion impedes economic success. However, Bangaru Laxman, a *Dalit* politician, was a prominent member of the *Hindutva* movement. Another political issue is *Dalit* affirmative-action quotas in government jobs and university admissions. About 8 per cent of the seats in the National and State Parliaments are reserved for Scheduled Caste and Scheduled Tribe candidates.

Jagjivan Ram (1908-1986) was the first Scheduled Caste leader to emerge at the national level from Bihar. He was member of the Constituent Assembly that drafted India's Constitution. His last position in government was as Deputy Prime Minister of India in the Janata Party government of 1977-1979. In modern times, several Bharatiya Janata Party leaders were *Dalits*, including Dinanath Bhaskar, Ramchandra Veerappa and Dr. Suraj Bhan. In India's most populous state, Uttar Pradesh, *Dalits* have had a major political impact. The *Dalit*-led Bahujan Samaj Party (BSP) had previously run the government and that party's leader, Mayawati, served several times as Chief Minister. Regarding her election in 2007, some reports claimed her victory was due to her ability to win support from both 17 per cent of Muslims and nearly 17 per cent Brahmins alongside 80 per cent of *Dalits*. However, surveys of voters on the eve of elections, indicated that caste loyalties were not the voters' principal concern. Instead, inflation and other issues of social and economic development dictated the outcome.[28] Mayawati's success in reaching across castes has led to speculation about her as a potential future Prime Minister of India. Aside from Mayawati in Uttar Pradesh, Damodaram Sanjivayya was Chief Minister of Andhra Pradesh, from 11 January, 1960 — 12 March, 1962 and Jitan Ram Majhi was Chief Minister of Bihar for just less than a year. In 1997, K.R. Narayanan, who was a *Dalit*, was elected as President of India. There is no such category leader retrieve till now. Even before 1964 was not present any Politbeuro member in CPIM party. Vote bank politics are common in India, usually based on religion or caste. Indeed, the term itself was coined by the Indian sociologist, M.N. Srinivas.[29] The Political Resolution of the 18th Congress of the CPI(M) held in 2005 gives concrete guidance to the Party to take up caste and social issues. In the section titled "Caste Oppression and Dalits", it says, "The caste system contains both social oppression and class exploitation. The *Dalits* suffer from both types of exploitation in the worst form. 86.25 per cent of the Scheduled Caste households are landless and 49 per cent of the Scheduled Castes in the rural areas are agricultural workers. Communists who champion abolition of the caste system, eradication of untouchability and caste oppression have to be in the forefront in launching struggles against the denial of basic human rights. This struggle has to be combined with the struggle to end the landlord-dominated order which consigns the *Dalit* rural masses to bondage. The issues of land, wages and employment must be taken up to unite different sections of the working people and the non-*Dalit* rural poor must be made conscious of the evils of caste oppression and discrimination by a powerful democratic campaign. There are some *Dalit* organizations and NGOs who seek to foster anti-Communist feelings amongst the *Dalit* masses and to detach them from the Left movement. Such sectarian and, in certain cases, foreign-funded activities must be countered and exposed by positively putting forth the Party's stand on caste oppression and making special efforts to draw the *Dalit* masses into common struggles."[30] There have been instances where it has been alleged that an election-winning party reneged on promises made to the *Dalits* made during the election campaign or have excluded them from party affairs. In the time of Left front Government in West Bengal, a lot of *Dalit* leaders were not available. Kanti Biswas, Upen Kisku and some other *Dalit* leaders were present there. But maximum *Dalit* voters were the supporter of the left front Government.

Conclusion

In 1991, 70 per cent of the total SC households were landless or near landless (owning less than one acre). This increased to 75 per cent in 2000. In 1991, 13 per cent of the rural SC households were landless. However, in 2000 this saw a decline and was 10 per cent. As per the Agricultural Census of 1995-96, the bottom 61.6 per cent of operational holdings accounted for only 17.2 per cent of the total operated land area. As against this, the top 7.3 per cent of operational holdings accounted for 40.1 per cent of the total operated area. This gives an indication of land concentration in the hands of a few. In 2000, about 28 per cent of SC households in rural areas had acquired some access to fixed capital assets (agricultural land and non-land assets). This was only half compared to 56 per cent for other non-SC/ST households who had some access to fixed capital assets. In the urban areas, the proportion was 27 per cent for SCs and 35.5 per cent for others. In 2000, 49.06 per cent of the working SC population were agricultural labourers, as compared to 32.69 per cent for the STs and only 19.66 per cent for the others. This shows the preponderance of *Dalits* in agricultural labour. Between 1991 and 2001, the number of agricultural labourers in India increased from 7.46 crore to 10.74 crore, and a large proportion of them were *Dalits*.[31] As a result, providing elementary education, basic health services and ensuring nutritious food to *Dalit* has become far-away dream. In short, with the implementation of the package of globalization, India may become more prosperous with 9 per cent GDP growth rate, but it will not emerge as a just and equitable society. The divide between the people — the upper and poor will widen further, sharpening the stratification that already exists in our society. A large number of *Dalits* have been benefited with various schemes of the government such as SCP (Special Component Plan), NSFDC (National Scheduled Castes Finance Development Corporation), MSY (Mahila Samridhi Yojana), NSKFDC (National Safai Karmachari Finance Development Corporation) etc. which in time have brought economic prosperity among them. Presently, SCs students are availing the facilities like Ashram Hostel, Book Grant, Scholarship, Education loan etc. It is the impact of socio-economic and political globalization in India. According to Mondal Commission, near about figure of *Dalits* are 85 per cent in India and 98 per cent are poor among 85 per cent of *Dalits*. Moreover, taking the reservation and other facilities 2-3 per cent are creamy layer or rich among them.[32]

NOTES

1. Hardtmann Eva-Maria, *The Dalit Movement in India* (Local practices, Global Connections), Oxford University Press, 2009, New Delhi, p. x.
2. *Ibid.*, pp. 185-86.
3. PhD thesis by Pradip Chauhan, *Social Status of Scheduled Castes of Maldah District*, p. 73.
4. *Ibid.*, p. 73.
5. *Status of Caste System in Modern India*, Ambedkar.org. 2004, pp. 34-35.
6. *BBC News*, 16 July, 2009 and *NCHRO*, 2009.
7. Singh, Darshan (2009), "Development of Scheduled Castes in India — A Review", *Journal of Rural Development*, 28(4): 529-42. Archived from the original on 22 December, 2010.
8. *www.dnaindia.com* "Dalits in India are Poorer than Muslims: Government Report", *DNA*, 7 November, 2014 and *www.scroll.in*, Mukunth, Vasudevan. "Who Among India's Young are Likely to Become Modern Slaves?"

9. Daily, Lisa A., *Constructing a New Nationalism from Below: The Dalit Movement, Politics and Transnational Networking* (2009). Graduate Theses and Dissertations. https://scholarcommons.usf.edu/etd/1920, pp. 36-37.
10. Sengupta, Somini (29 August, 2008). "Crusader Sees Wealth as Cure for Caste Bias", *The New York Times*, India, Retrieved 20 November, 2011 and Wax, Emily (31 August, 2008). "In an Indian Village, Signs of the Loosening Grip of Caste", *The Washington Post*, Retrieved 20 November, 2011.
11. Census Report 2011, *The Indian Express*, 6 July, 2015. Retrieved 6 September, 2015.
12. *The Times of India*, 28 October, 2012. Retrieved 13 September, 2015.
13. PhD thesis by Pradip Chauhan, *Social Status of Scheduled Castes of Maldah District*, p. 73.
14. *The Indian Express*, 27 May, 2002. Retrieved 27 September, 2002.
15. Zelliet, Eleanor, "India's Dalits: Racism and Contemporary Change", *Global Dialogue*, 12(2), Archived from the original, on 30 April, 2013.
16. Klostermaier, Klaus, *A Survey of Hinduism: Third Edition*, State University of New York Press, p. 297.
17. Zelliet, Eleanor, "India's Dalits: Racism and Contemporary Change", *Global Dialogue*, 12(2), Archived from the original, on 30 April, 2013.
18. Sengupta, Somini (29 August, 2008). "Crusader Sees Wealth as Cute for Caste Bias", *The New York Times*, India. Retrieved 20 November, 2011.
19. Bhandare, Namita (5 December, 2014). "Casteism Exists in India, Let's not Remain in Denial", *The Hindustan Times*, Archived from the original on 15 December, 2014.
20. Chishti, Seema (29 November, 2014). "Biggest Caste Survey: One in Four Indians Admit to Practicing Untouchability", *The Indian Express*. Retrieved 30 July, 2017.
21. *Census Report 2011.*
22. Sarkar, Sravani (5 December, 2014). "Children Bear the Brunt of Caste Abuse in Rural Areas", *The Hindustan Times*, Archived from the original on 13 December, 2014.
23. Lama, Prawesh (7 December, 2011). "Dalit Professor Harassed for SC Quata Reforms Thesis". *India Today*, Retrieved 24 July, 2017 and *Business Standard*, Press Trust of India, 28 March, 2015.
24. Sarkar, Sravani (5 December, 2014). "Children Bear the Brunt of Caste Abuse in Rural Areas", *The Hindustan Times*. Archived from the original on 13 December, 2014.
25. Manvir Saini, TNN (29 July, 2015). *The Times of India*. Retrieved 6 September, 2015.
26. Gupta, Dipankar, *Interrogating Caste; Understanding Hierarchy and Difference in India Society*, Penguin, New Delhi, 2000, p. 157.
27. *Daily News and Analysis*, 3 June, 2012. Retrieved 20 January, 2013.
28. *The Hindu*, India, 14 March, 2007. Retrieved 20 November, 2011.
29. Harshe, Rajen (2008). "Thinking about Democracy, Identity Politics and Development in India", in Brar, Bhupinder; Kumar, Ashutosh; Ram, Ronki (eds.), *Globalization and the Politics of Identity in India*, Pearson Education India, pp. 205, 279. Dalits are often used as a vote bank.
30. The Political Resolution of the 18th Congress of the CPI(M) held in 2005.
31. *Census Report 1991 & 2001.*
32. Edited by Mondal, Dr. Chitta and Roymondal Dr. Prothama, *Banglar Dalit Andoloner Itibritto*, Kolkata, 2003, p. 401.

13

From Look East to Act East Policy
An Acceleration of India's Strategic Engagement with South-East Asia in 21st Century

Pankaj Kumar Mandal

India has political and cultural links with South-East Asian countries from the ancient period. To constitute stronger relation and to manage India's own economic crisis in 1990s, India initiated Look East approach towards South-East Asia. But surprisingly till the end of 2000 A.D., Look East was confined as an economic policy. Later in 2003, a second phase of Look East also declared but the strategic importance between India-ASEAN partnerships got less attention. Although the UPA-2 Government from 2012 had shown strategic commitment towards South-East Asian region but after the declaration of Act East Policy by P.M. Narendra Modi, a new shift in strategic partnership drew much attention. Hence in the present chapter, the recent status of strategic development between India and ASEAN has been studied. Strategic cooperation is supposed to include all kinds of cooperation. The work is a study of how India is connected with ASEAN states in recent years through cultural diplomatic strategy, defence, security and economy related strategy and cyber technical understanding etc. In this context, it is also shown how India is operating its strategic mechanism with ASEAN organization and individually towards each ASEAN member with bi-lateral, multilateral process through the utilization of soft and hard power initiatives. Before discussing the chapter in details let us look into a very brief literature review.

Literature Review

In the year 2006, Sanjaya Baru had written *Strategic Consequences of*

India's Economic Performance, Academic Foundation, New Delhi, 2006. This writing was only about economic outcome of solid Indian financial world. But it is clear from a mere statistics that since 2009 China was largest trading partner of ASEAN while in the year 2008 India was seventh biggest trading partner. So, India was a dwarf concerning Chinese economic strategy. Another scholar S.D. Muni also argues future *Strategic Dimension of Look East Policy* but not constituted any holistic design of strategic understanding between India and ASEAN countries (*Muni's working paper no. 121, Institute of South-East Asian Studies, Singapore, February 2011*). Ambassador Rajiv Sikri, in his book (*Challenge and Strategy, Rethinking Indian Foreign Policy*, Sage Publication, 2009) discussed ASEAN zone as an arc of prosperity and also emphasized on economic strategic dimension of the region. In the year 2013, 28th June, Center for Strategic and International Studies published a paper which was edited by Ted Osius & C. Rajamohan (*Enhancing India ASEAN Connectivity*) has stressed on ASEAN-USA-INDIA trio connectivity which can be made effective to a shift of power in Asia. In a recent book, Yang Xiaoping has been advised to incorporate China with India's Act East Vision to reach a win-win situation (*Look East to Act East Policy*, ed. by Gurudas Das and Joshua Thomas, Routledge, 2016). But in my opinion, China might not be a dependable friend for India as long they would help Pakistan. All those literatures did not give a clear outlook of strategic partnership between India and ASEAN member countries and had not been discussed major imperatives of strategy related to India-ASEAN relations. After 25 years of the establishment of Look East Policy, it is a suitable time to critique the past and make projections for the next decade.

Firstly, we can say, towards South-East Asia, some effective key aspects of India's strategic construct are: 1. Maintenance of coastal security, 2. Combating piracy, 3. Intelligence sharing and counter terrorism, 4. Protection of the legitimate sovereign use of international waters, 5. Act as deterrence to traditional and non-traditional threats, 6. Maintain safety, security and stability in the region, 7. Establish peace and encourage greater cooperation, 8. Enforcement of international law, 9. Disaster relief operations, 10. Conservation of marine environment, joint action against climate change, 11. Build of an effective security architecture, 12. Expanding cultural diplomatic strategy, 13. Cooperation in cyber knowledge exchange, science progress, technological exchange, 14. Exchange of strategic ideas for reciprocal interests to fight terrorism, illegal narcotics trade, human trafficking.

Strong initiatives are being started to take in the time of NDA-2 Government mainly focusing on those above areas.

Secondly, Act East Policy is a power boost to implement both hard and soft power understanding for strategic benefits. It is also suggested to maintain assertive maritime strategy to check and balance the rising Chinese blue water navy. Till the end of 2016, ASEAN countries mainly are being focused on East Asia, pacific zone while the Indian Ocean region can be a geographical centre of gravity for ASEAN members. Simultaneously, India has to set up a clear military mechanism in order to maintain peace and solidarity in Bay of Bengal and Asia Pacific Zone. Chinese growing influence in South-East Asia also become an issue of concern for India. A country in control of China region would be a direct threat to India's security because many South-East Asian states have adjoining land and sea borders with India. In this connection, the researcher argues that India should not support One-China Policy; otherwise the cunning of One-China can grasp the whole South-China region.

Thirdly, it is obvious that India-ASEAN strategic groupings can make impact on international system. This power orbit strategically started to reap crops from Asia-Pacific Zone or from regional or sub-regional groupings like — BIMSTEC, MEKONG-GANGA initiatives or SCO. Moreover, India can make deal of nuclear energy and build up nuclear non-proliferation jointly with Australia and ASEAN. Because North Korea, China and Japan are enriched with good potential of nuclear weapons and the declaration of 'nuclear free zone' by ASEAN may not be sustained in near future.

From last two decades of twentieth century end of Cold War, collapse of USSR, rise of China, India's subsequent economic liberalization, the rise of ASEAN as regional power surprised the world. Indian Prime Minister Narasimha Rao's initiatives regarding "Look East Policy" were a triumph card to accelerate India's relationship with South-East Asian States. In the year 1997, India started to share 1500 kilometres international border with ASEAN because in the meantime Myanmar became an active member state of ASEAN organization. This incident added strategic food for thinking better India ASEAN Partnership. ASEAN countries have realized that it is in their interest to include India in a regional cooperative effort to observe India's strength. In this context, one of the objectives of the Framework Agreement on Comprehensive Economic Cooperation signed between ASEAN and India is to facilitate the more effective economic integration of the new ASEAN member states and the bridging of development hiatus among the relations. India's willingness to accede to the Treaty of Amity and Cooperation in South-East Asia and its endorsement of the South-East Asia Nuclear Weapons Free Zone has further assured the ASEAN countries. Moreover to a large extent ASEAN also appreciates India's security concerns which are due to geopolitical reasons rather than any hegemonic aspirations.

India became a sectorial dialogue partner of ASEAN in 1992, which was upgraded to full dialogue partnership in 1996. India's decision to accede to the 1976 ASEAN Treaty of Amity and Cooperation in July 2003 was considered a major milestone. The First Indo-ASEAN Summit in Phnom Penh in November 2002 institutionalized ASEAN-India relations and is seen as the success of India's Look East Policy and as an appreciation of India's emergence as an important player in the Asia Pacific Region. Since 2002, annual Summits are being organized with ASEAN. India and ASEAN celebrated the 20th anniversary of dialogue-level partnership and the anniversary of Summit-level partnership with a Commemorative Summit in New Delhi under the theme 'ASEAN-India Partnership for Peace and Shared Prosperity' in December 2012. The Commemorative Summit endorsed taking the partnership to the next level of 'Strategic Partnership'.

From the first decades of 21st Century, India-ASEAN Cooperation scattered in multi-dimensional sectors including agriculture, culture, environment, human resource development, health and pharmaceuticals, information and communication technology, new and renewable energy, space science, science and technology, telecommunications, transport and infrastructure, tourism and trade. In the year 2009, India announced a contribution of US$ 50 million to India-ASEAN Cooperation Fund to support implementation of the India-ASEAN Plan of Action 2010-2015 which calls for further deepening and intensifying of India-ASEAN cooperation in the political, economic and socio-cultural sectors. The ASEAN-India Centre was a milestone in this relationship which established in New Delhi in June 2013. In the economic field, total trade increased from 2.9 billion in 1993 to 47.5 billion in 2008, on the another hand India ASEAN bilateral trade grew from a meagre $7.06 billion in 2000-01 to a massive $78.9 billion in 2011-12 while it declined to $65 billion in 2015-16. After that it witnessed growth revival to $71.6 billion in 2016-17. India's share of total ASEAN trade quadrupled from just 0.7 per cent in 1993 to 2.8 per cent in 2008, making it ASEAN's seventh biggest trade partner. India has also signed bilateral free trade agreements with Singapore and Thailand and sub-regional initiatives like the Mekong-Ganga Cooperation Initiative (MGCI) and the Bay of Bengal Initiative for Multi-Sectorial Technical and Economic Cooperation (BIMSTEC). ASEAN and India have also concluded a Free Trade Agreement in Goods (AIFTA), which was concluded in May 2009. It became fully operational from 1 August, 2011 when the process of ratification by all the ASEAN countries was completed.

Trade between India and ASEAN was worth about $76 billion in 2012-13. Both sides have set a target of increasing this to $100 billion by 2015. Further, the Ministry of Commerce and Industry, Government of India organized the 2nd ASEAN-India Business Fair from December in 2012. India is also part of ASEAN's fresh initiative for negotiation for a pan-Indo-Pacific economic integration involving sixteen founding members of the East Asia Summit (ten ASEAN states and six dialogue partners — Australia, China, India, Japan, South Korea and New Zealand), known as Regional Comprehensive Economic Partnership. In the 4th India-ASEAN Tourism Ministers Meeting held in Vientiane in January 2013, a Protocol to amend the MOU on Strengthening Tourism Cooperation between ASEAN and India was signed and the ASEAN-India tourism website (*www.indiaasean.org*) was launched. Facility of 'Visa on arrival' was extended to 7 ASEAN countries — Cambodia, Indonesia, Laos, Myanmar, Singapore, the Philippines and Vietnam. Cooperation between India and ASEAN is also being intensified in the cultural, educational and academic fields, through the promotion of people-to-people contacts, and ongoing initiatives such as the Youth Exchange Programme, Media Exchange Programme, and Special Training Courses for ASEAN Diplomats and Eminent Persons Lecture Series. India has established Centres for English Language Training and Entrepreneurship Development Centres in Cambodia, Laos PDR, Myanmar and Vietnam.

India played a crucial role in setting up of the Mekong-Ganga Cooperation Project in 2000 which includes India and the five ASEAN countries including the four newer ASEAN members — Vietnam, Laos, Cambodia, Myanmar and Thailand. The India-ASEAN Science & Technology Fund was set up in 2007 with an initial corpus of US$ 1 million and the India-ASEAN Green Fund was also established in 2007 with US$ 5 million for funding pilot projects to promote adaptation and mitigation technologies in the field of climate change. The Ministry of Environment and Forests convened the first Meeting of the India-ASEAN Environment Ministers in New Delhi which was followed by an India-ASEAN Workshop on Capacity Building. The first India-ASEAN Ministerial Meeting on New and Renewable Energy was also convened in November 2012. Likewise, the first meeting of the Heads of Space Agencies of India and ASEAN member countries was held in Bangalore to discuss cooperation in the space sector. India and ASEAN also share concern on non-traditional security challenges in the areas of climate change and natural disaster relief. An India-ASEAN Expert Meeting on Climate Change was organized at the Indian Institute of Science, Bangalore in 2012. The area of science and technology offers great scope for India and ASEAN to cooperate. Both India and ASEAN can take advantage of each other's strength. ASEAN has significant hardware and manufacturing capabilities while India has software and services capabilities.

The increasing importance of maritime trade and energy security for India has made it imperative to ensure the safety of Sea Lanes of Communication in South-East Asia. In this context, ASEAN and India can cooperate in the sharing of intelligence and technologies as enshrined in the 2003 ASEAN-India Joint Declaration on Cooperation to Combat International Terrorism. From 1990s India has been cooperating with the military establishments of South-East Asian countries. India and Malaysia signed a memorandum of agreement on defence cooperation in 1993 under which India began to train the air force personnel of Malaysia. In 2003, India and Singapore signed a bilateral defence cooperation agreement which furthered India's training of Singapore Military personnel. Since then India has given Singapore a wider access to training facilities in India. Besides India Vietnam strategic relation also strengthened till 2016. India also has taken a positive role in South China Sea dispute.

India needs to be credible strategic Partner of South-East Asian countries with equal and similar status notions. India's big brothership idea of foreign policy is now backdated. What India done in South Asia region would not be juxtaposed with South-East Asia region. Hence, Act East Policy should be a great leap forward regarding strategic partnership with ASEAN countries for coming decades. In response to expansionist Chinese policy, from its string of pearls strategy, one belt one road etc. and increasing Naval presence in the South China Sea and the Indian Ocean region, New Delhi also decided to initiate more strategic dialogues and military exercises with ASEAN states. In the year 2018, ASEAN India commemorative summit was held in New Delhi remembering the 25 years of its constructive engagement which was an instance of bonding the strength of India and ASEAN communities. Hopefully at the 14th ASEAN India summit in Vientiane in September 2016, Prime Minister Modi highlighted the multi-dimensional nature of India-ASEAN relationship, evoking stronger grounds for rejuvenated

'Act East Policy' in India's foreign policy initiatives. In a nutshell, we can say India's strategic relation with ASEAN is intensified in a positive way in 2019. We can expect that the "Acche Din" would be continued regarding India-ASEAN strategic relationship in near future.

REFERENCES

A. Parthasarthy, "The Gains of Looking East", *The Pioneer*, New Delhi: 21 November, 2002.

Amitabh Matto, "ASEAN in India's Foreign Policy", in Frederic Grare and Amitabh Matto eds., *India and ASEAN: The Politics of India's Look East Policy*, New Delhi: Manohar.

Amitav Acharya, *Constructing a Security Community in South-East Asia: ASEAN and the Problem of Regional Order*, Routledge, 2009.

C. Raja Mohan, *Crossing the Rubicon: The Shaping of India's New Foreign Policy*, New York: Palgrave Macmillan, 2004.

C. Raja Mohan, "India and the Balance of Power", *Foreign Affairs Journal*, 85(4), 17-32, 2006.

D.R. Sardesai, *South-East Asia: Past and Present*, 6th edition, Westview Press, 2010.

Frederic Grare, "In Search of a Role: India and the ASEAN Regional Forum", in Frederic Grare and Amitabh Matto (eds), *India and ASEAN: The Politics of India's Look East Policy*, New Delhi: Manohar, 2001.

G.V.C. Naidu, "ASEAN: Challenges Ahead and Implications for India", *Strategic Analyses*, Vol. XXIII, No. 2 pp. 283-97.

India and ASEAN: Security Paradigm AD 2000, Speech by Mr. Jaswant Singh, External Affairs Minister, Singapore, 2 June, 2000.

Isabelle Saint-Mezard, "The Look East Policy: An Economic Perspective", in Frederic Grare and Amitabh Matto (eds), *Beyond the Rhetoric: The Economics of India's Look East Policy*, New Delhi: Manohar, 2003.

Jayanta Kumar Ray, *India's Foreign Relations 1947-2007*, New Delhi: Routledge, 2011.

Kripa Sridharan, *The ASEAN Region in India's Foreign Policy*, Alder Shot, UK, Dartmouth Publishing.

Mansingh, Dilip Lahiri, J.N. Dixit, Bhabani Sen Gupta, Sujatha Singh and Ashok Sajjanhar (eds), *Indian Foreign Policy: Agenda for the 21st Century*, New Delhi: Konark Publishers.

Ministry of External Affairs, *Annual Report 2010-2015*, retrieved from http://www.meaindia.nic.in. Govt. of India Publication, New Delhi, 2016.

Parimal Kumar Das, Ed., *The Troubled Region: Issues of Peace and Development in South-East Asia*, New Delhi: Sage Publications, 1987.

Rajiv Sikri, *Challenge and Strategy, Rethinking Indian Foreign Policy*, Sage Publication, 2009.

Sanjaya Baru, *Strategic Consequences of India's Economic Performance*, New Delhi: Academic Foundation, 2006.

T.N. Kaul, *India and Indo-China: Perspectives of Cooperation*, New Delhi: Patriot Publishers, 1987.

Tridib Chakrabarti, "Unraveling India's ASEAN Policy", in Anjali Ghosh, ed., *India's Foreign Policy*, Mumbai: Pearson Education, 2003.

V.P. Dutt, *India's Foreign Policy*, New Delhi: Radiant Publishers, 1985.

14

Impact of Globalization on the Politics and Culture of the State of West Bengal

Saswati Das

The process of uniting the modern world is called globalization. The process of uniting the whole world is called globalization.[1] Form international relations readers to expert scholars, the word globalization has been and is being discussed in various parts of India, such as in educational institutions, industry and commerce etc. From all these seminars and detailed discussions, it is evident that the lives of ordinary people are closely related to their livelihood. That is why people at all levels are particularly interested in globalization. In particular the context of the impact of the Third World economy and social system is more important. Globalization has naturally inspired people to be involved in life and livelihood.

Aims and Objectives of the Research

In my first research paper, I have tried to outline how globalization has affected the state politics of West Bengal and outline its extraterrestrial and international evolution.

The "World" Form of Globalization: The Nature of the State, Organization and Globalization

Globalization is a widely used concept in current world politics. On the one hand, globalization sheds light on the changing nature of the world system, on the other hand, sheds light on the changing nature of functional political and economic relations within the world system. Although the term "World" is very old, the concept of globalization derived from it began to be used in the 1960s. Professor Ronald Robertson is the promoter of the concept of globalization. He formalized and defined the first globalization. He wanted to present the discussion of modernization of sociology in an international context.[2] According to Robertson, globalization as an idea refers to the idea of making the world compressed on the one hand, and the idea of uniting the world on the other. That is, globalization highlights the growing interdependence of trade, military and cultural fields between different countries of the world. But the most important aspect of the concept of globalization is "One world."[3]

Anthony Giddnes, in defining globalization, says that globalization is such a strong factor of social relations round the world that local life in remote areas is being affected by events that take place hundreds of miles away.[4] This definition of Giddnes emphasizes the changes that are taking place in social relations not only internationally but also locally. Globalization refers to a new kind of policy or strategy by which the former imperialist and capitalist countries try to re-establish their economic and cultural domination and exploitation. Basically, globalization is a conspiracy of the capitalist countries whose purpose is to exert an irresistible influence on the economic, social and cultural system of Third World politics and the people of developing countries. Since it is not possible to maintain special colonies or colonies, the capitalist countries have adopted new strategies to adapt to the new situation in order to maintain their economic exploitation. As a result, it has adopted only the strategic aspect of exploitation. This has only changed the strategic aspect of exploitation. But the effort and strategy to re-establish the old economic system has come to be known as the globalization of international terminology. Some experts call globalization or economic neo-colonialism an "old wine in a new bottle."[5] The influence of Western or Western thought, especially in the Third World, is at the heart of the Western concept and the process of globalization has evolved in two ways — liberalization and privatization.

The Economy of Globalization, The Globalization of the Economy: Some Special Aspects of Democratic Processing

Now India could not live without being a member of the new world economic system and family. We know that after the year of the path shown by Prime Minister Nehru. As a goal in the socio-economic field of independent India, Nehru declared the establishment of an egalitarian socialist pattern of society. To that end, Nehru did not see any path to unbridled capitalism and orthodox socialist economy as a strategy for economic development. Rather he adopted a Mixed Economy as the third of these two paths. There are two more aspects of Nehru's model: 1. Parliamentary democracy in the political arena which is based on universal adult suffrage. 2. Bureaucratic management of the West Minster Model in the administrative field.[6]

Naturally, the cornerstone of the mixed economy was laid in the 1948 industrial policy. In 1950, the State Controlled Planning Commission was formed. In 1956, a third party followed compromise between socialist style socialist economics, known as mixed economics. In this economy, both state enterprises and private enterprises are given the opportunity to work and play a role. However, very important areas were left in the hands of government initiatives. Less important sectors such as agriculture, daily necessities and services were taken over by the private sector. But since 1980, a bleak picture of India's economic situation has emerged. Inflation rises sharply and the population continues to rise unabated. The number of unemployed youth continues to rise. July 24, 1991 will be marked as a historic day in the Indian economy. Because, on the same day Manmohan Singh, the Finance Minister in the Narasimha Rao government, announced a New Economic Policy that marked the beginning of a long 40 years departure from Nehru's socio-economic development policy. The free market economy was introduced in India through this new economic reform — Privatization of government enterprises and globalization of the econcmy.

Impact of Globalization on the State Politics and Political Culture of West Bengal Process and Nature of Technology and Administrative Processing

West Bengal is no exception where it will be free from the effects of globalization. The impact of globalization on the political and political cultural spheres of West Bengal is far reaching. The use of information technology is the working of political parties in West Bengal in the formulation of public relations policy etc. As a result, the political and cultural form of West Bengal has become a process of IT based governance. The progress or aggression of globalization has hurt the old notion of public administration. The call for a free world market, the unstoppable progress of electronic government has necessitated a change in the old notion of state government management theory. Demands for participatory management and flexible administrative structures have been organized to reinvent the government. Some questions have been raised in the debate as to whether the state public administration should be people-centric or capital-centric or the nature or size of the state government will change etc. The first satellite connections were made in 1970s. Imperialism neo-colonial ever forced house wives to wear Manchester clothes, cold water has once again poisoned developing countries. But, the disorder that infected the world in the 1990s in the name of globalization is its first symptom of rapid international investment system. Multinational corporations continue to play the most important role as carries of this disease.[8] The market oriented government policy adopted by the national and state governments has increased the potential for global market expansion not only this, the former thinking of the nation-state has also changed. New investment policy, loose trade policy, technology exchange and consumerist economy, a new world culture has emerged, breaking the barrier of state culture that the revolution has established in the world of information technology. The first implication of this complex and multifaceted change were the rapid development of technology in the last half of the twentieth century, the idea of electronic government and the consequent results. The revolutionary development of communication and information technology in West Bengal has revolutionized the world market and especially the administration.

Globalization has marked a revolutionary change in the nature and scope of public administration. Public administration has been forced to adapt to the new economic trends in its application and reading. Good governance has been implemented at the administrative level of West Bengal by equating efficient and efficient management and rapid development management. The E-Governance or IT-based governance process has not only gained popularity in the West Bengal administration and it has become inevitable. E-Governance is the use of information technology in government activities to achieve the goals of the organization's authority. There has been talk of SMART governance in this information-based governance process. The feature of SMART GOVERNANCE is — S = Simple, M = Moral, A = Accountable, R = Responsive and T = Transparent. These are just some of the goal setting shareware that you can use — 1. Exchange of information between citizen, government departments and business groups. 2. Recognize speed and efficiency in the delivery of government services. 3. Improving internal skills. 4. Decrease in expenditure and increase in revenue. 5. Restructuring in the administrative process. 6. Development of quality of services.

The World Bank is talking about providing fast service to the citizens through internet and computer through the introduction of governance. The key is efficient governance, empowerment of citizens, reduction of corruption and increase in transparency. E-Governance helps citizens communicate with the government, reflecting their needs.[9]

In India, Information Technology Act, 2000 and Semiconductor Integrated Circuits Layout Design Act, 2000 are approved to make the administrative process information based. The Information Technology Act has made it possible to recognize electronic documents, legal validity of digital signatures, preservation of electronic records, publication of electronic gazettes etc. Growing progress of E-Governance in West Bengal maintains momentum in governance process. The IT-based governance process in West Bengal facilitates interaction and exchange of information among all participants in the society. This process can be noticed in the relationship between the government to government (G2G).This relationship can be horizontal in the exchange of information or communication between different government agencies. However, stratification in the national administration can also be vertical communication. That is, the vertical relationship between the national government, regional government, local government and their respective level departments and divisions can be observed. But the primary goal of this communication and exchange relationship is to ensure efficiency, effectiveness and results.

Maintaining the communication of citizens with the government (G2C) is one of the aspects of IT based governance process. As a result, there is a lot of transparency and awareness on the part of the government in providing any service to the citizens. Citizens can know where, when, how, government services will be available.

In this case internet, social media, phone etc. can be talked about. G2C is clearly observed in the administrative system of West Bengal. The impact of globalization in West Bengal is another dynamic of the IT-based governance process with the business community working with the government (G2B). The old file-based system and stratification have created bureaucratic red tape, making it difficult to do business and make quick decisions. The use of information technology allows the business community to operate independently and efficiently in the field of licensing, tax collection and communication. In the political context of West Bengal, the use of the internet and computers has signalled a revolutionary shift in public service and administration. The direct contact of the people with the government, the far-reaching impact of globalization on government policy formulation, implementation, natural disaster response, and ever prevention of corruption is far-reaching. In the multi-party system of West Bengal, one of the ways to present political rivalries and election campaigns, programmes of political parties, to the people is through this IT-based governance process.

The Mixed Character of the Political Culture of India Stunning Innovations and Debater on Globalization, Indications of the Revolutions Direction in Technology, Modernity and Tradition, Values and Overall Life Consciousness

There are various resources behind the complete development of this mixed character of the political culture of India. One of the main sources of this is that, people of different religions, castes, class, professions and languages live side by side. Due to the diversity of race, religion, caste, class, profession and language, the political beliefs and values by the people have different character. As a result, the political beliefs of the rich class are very different from the normal beliefs due to class differences. In the same way, there are still some differences in the political beliefs and values of the Hindu and Muslim people, there are also political beliefs and attitude among the Hindi-speaking, Urdu-speaking, Tamil-speaking, Punjabi-speaking, Bengali-speaking people. Moreover due to the regional diversity, there are different political beliefs, among the people of different regions. For this reaction, there is a big difference between the political consequences of South India on the mentality of the people of East India and the people of West India. Similarly, a mixed political and cultural environment observed in West Bengal. Another source or reason for the main character of this political culture is the simultaneous interest in tradition and antiquity while the impact of globalization is a touch of contemporary modernity. Although there is an interest in tradition or antiquity in the rural areas of West Bengal, this is now a touch of modernity in the villages; on the other hand, modern western oriented lifestyle has become active in industrialized urban areas. Although respect for this tradition and traditional way of life is still present in the city to some extent.

On the other hand, in line with the existing feudal system in India, the modern industrial-rich capitalist system is still in place. Therefore, it is seen that industrialization and urbanization, civilization and Westernization are taking place at a very fast pace by utilizing science and technology, globalization has led to unprecedented revolution in industry and agriculture and far reaching improvement in trade, transportation, education, medicine, scientific research, nuclear testing and so on as a result secularism in India, universal suffrage issuance of pictorial identity cards to voters in fair elections, sense of national solidarity, rights and duties, important aspects of modern life-oriented consciousness have been gently developed. In his book '*Politics in India*' eminent researcher and eminent thinker Rajani Kothari while analyzing the nature of the political culture formed on the basis of the interconnectedness between the traditional way of life and the modern lifestyle, has shown with great conviction that the modern lifestyle of India is modern. This is a strong existence and the fullness of India's political culture cannot be found at all without one of these two life-styles. So, he says objectively, firmly and transparently that, "Those who are modernized as a rejection of tradition, their model does not apply to India (Political Culture)" similarly, the Rudolph Couple, in their book '*Modernity of Tradition: Political Development in India*' says that the political culture of India is enhanced by following modernity while not abandoning tradition and antiquity.[10]

As a result of globalization and information technology revolution, India like other countries of the world is facing information revolution. Unprecedented advanced in the internet, mobile phone, iPods, satellites, televisions, radios and printing presses have led to the emergence of the information society or Network society. The sophisticated demands of activism and transparency in the municipal society are now about to break down the closed wall of real information. The Right to Information Act is designed to break down the walls of privacy. Karl W. Deutsch has identified these media as 'The Nerves of Government'.[11] Statistical information through the media drivers the flow of events and politics. Perhaps Tolstoy said that the ignorance of the people is the power of government. The conventional method of keeping people ignorant is to hide and distort information and the media has a big role in the implementation of this method. Advertising on sponsorship gives profit to the media. So the owner cannot do any irrational work that can turn off the source of advertising or sponsorship. It is the job of the journalist to follow the instructions of the employer. The owner's decision is always profit oriented. Editorial policy is the boastful name of the owner. With their real prospective in mind we need to reach for truth.

India is now ranked third in the world terms of internet usage. In this country of 100 million internet users, the trend of political debate on social networking sites has increased significantly. Political parties have emphasized on net promotion by setting up their own websites or joining Facebook, and Twitter. In India, the initial impact on liberalization, privatization, globalization and the media has been on consumerism. Now-a-days, more than media news, there is a tendency to serve sensational news. Everything is now a game of 'hype' creation, everyone involved in the rat race to increase TRPR circulation. Many people are worried about the sound of the TV and the explosion of speech.

There is always a search on television for something extraordinary that is something extraordinary from television that is exceptional. Everything that is out of the routine, out of the daily routine, is being explored. There is also another consonant to the exceptional which must be different from other channels. So, one terrible pressure works to be exclusive. This results in distorted information, drama and misrepresentation that mislead the public. This statement in the news service goes through the politics of editing. Maxwell media mentions four types of 'bias' such as —

1. **Partisan bias:** Directly supporting a political party in the editorial.
2. **Propaganda bias:** Propaganda is run while serving information.
3. **Unwritten bias:** In this bias, the journalist or correspondent subconsciously expresses a particular point of view.
4. **Ideological bias:** To give precedence to anyone ideology.[12]

The influence of corporate house on the media is growing worldwide. The existence of media depends on advertising, so the news has to be served in such a way that ensures the favour of the advertiser. A huge change in the Indian media is inevitable in the last century. Globalization has led to the expansion of the Indian middle class in the nineties of the last century. The media must continue to adapt to the new values and needs of this changing middle class. Satellite television is behind this change in the mentality of the middle class. Satellite television is challenging this nationalism beyond the borders of the state. When people in Karachi, Kolkata, Kathmandu and Khulna watch similar television programmes, a kind of election community is created. The impact of globalization on electoral conduct in West Bengal is determined by the "three Ms" in the language of the press. These are Media, Muscle Power and Money Power. Electoral behaviour is determined by a variety of complex elements, in which case it would be very simplistic to consider one element the main one. However, the communication revolution and the flood of information have given a new dimension to the election process. With so much excitement surrounding the election courtesy of the broadcast, the mood of the festival is rare in any other political system. Newspapers, magazines, radio and television channels are pre-election pooling to try to advance the polls. It was later found that almost every major media outlet took the help of polling. Exit polls are one of the most popular innovations in modern times. Exit polls have shown remarkable success in predicting election results. The impact of globalization on the electoral behaviour of the media is exactly the debate among researchers.[13]

Different Aspects of West Bengal Politics and Political Culture: Some Negative Commentary

However, the impact of this information technology on the politics and political culture of West Bengal has many negative aspects. The worst result of this new economy is unemployment. The new economy has created the biggest socio-economic political system by creating mountainous unemployment. As the new economy focuses on massive technical knowledge, employment opportunities have shrunk and unemployment is an economic disorder and a social curse. Another major disadvantage of this new economic policy is job insecurity, mass layoffs, voluntary retirement planning etc. The implementation of the new economy has not only initiated "jobless development" but also the voluntary retirement (VRS) and dismissal policy that has resulted in the temporization of labour. But in this case, the worker used to enjoy guaranteed social security.

Remnants of the Original Projection, An Appendix to Extraterrestrial and International Evolution

The use of technology in the administrative system of West Bengal, skilled human resources, information based awareness has developed among the people. However, despite the lack and disruption of internet services in remote villages, the profound impact of globalization can be seen in the state politics of West Bengal. In my first research paper, I have tried to outline how globalization has affected the state politics of West Bengal and its outward and international evolution.

NOTES

1. Sarkar, Kalyan Kumar, *Aadhunik Rastrabigyan*, Sree Bhumi Publishing House, 27th chapter, March 2012, p. 810.
2. Chakraborty, Radharaman, Chakraborty, Sukalpa, *Samosamoik Antorjatic Samporka*, Progressive Publication, 3rd chapter, November 2004, p. 116.
3. *Ibid.*, p. 117.
4. *Ibid.*
5. Ghosh, Nirmol Kanti Ghosh, Dr. Pritam, *Antorjatic Samporka*, Sree Bhumi Publishing House, 15th chapter, July 1995, p. 158.
6. Som, Dr. Subhas Chandra, *Janaprosason*, Calcutta Book House, 12th chapter, 1999, pp. 800-801.
7. *Ibid.*, p. 802.
8. Ghosh, Soma, *Janaprosason Tatto O Proyg*, Progressive Publication, 1st chapter, November 2004, p. 9.
9. Dey, Probir Kumar, Ghosh, Sraboni: *Janoprosasonar Dristivongi*, 1st Baishak, 1426, Kalyani Publishers, 6th chapter, p. 102.
10. Mukhopadhyay, Apurbomohan, Nandi, Dabasish, *Bharotio Rajniti*, Joy Durga Library, Bharatborser Rajnaitik Sanskriti, September 2011, pp. 278-79.
11. Mukhopadhyay, Apurbomohan, Nandi, Dabasish, *Bharotio Rajniti*, Joy Durga Library, Ganamadham o Bharotio Rajniti, September 2011, p. 288.
12. *Ibid.*, p. 291.
13. *Ibid.*, p. 293.

Section – IV

Environmental Aspects of Globalization

15

Mobile Radiations Causing Loss of Biodiversity
An Overview

Kantisree Goswami

Introduction

Globalization refers to the *integration* of markets in the global economy, leading to the increased *interconnectedness* of national economies. Markets where globalization is particularly significant include financial markets, such as capital markets, money and credit markets, and insurance markets, commodity markets, including markets for oil, coffee, tin, and gold, and product markets, such as markets for motor vehicles and consumer electronics. The globalization of sport and entertainment is also a feature of the late 20th and early 21st centuries.

The term *globalization* became popular in social science in the 1990s. It derives from the word *globalize*, which refers to the emergence of an international network of economic systems. The term 'globalization' had been used in its economic sense at least as early as 1981, and in other senses since at least as early as 1944. Theodore Levitt is credited with popularizing the term and bringing it into the mainstream business audience in the latter half of the 1980s. Sociologists Martin Albrow and Elizabeth King define globalization as "all those processes by which the people of the world are incorporated into a single world society."

Mobile Telephony: One of the Biggest Inventions of Globalization

Technology is one of the leading factors in the evolution of globalization. Technology has evolved to such an extent that mobile phones are used not only for family or business calls, but they are now a way of living. Mobile phones have become an important tool we can use anytime and anywhere and enable us to do various tasks all at the same time. As a portal for communications, messaging, entertainment and information, mobile phones have become the manifestation of the "digital age".

Some major ways in which mobile technologies enable globalization are:

- Expanding the productive opportunities of certain types of activities by enhancing social networks, reducing risks associated with employment seeking, and enabling freelance service work;
- Transforming and reinforcing the social and economic ties of micro-entrepreneurs and making local economies more efficient;
- Enabling mobility of businesses;
- Extending the capabilities of mobile phones to entrepreneurship, banking, e-learning, and health delivery systems; and
- Increasing the frequency of people's contact with friends, family, and existing business connections and facilitating new contacts with business partners, suppliers, and customers, no matter where they are.

Harmful Effects of Mobile Waves on Wild Flora and Fauna: Disturbing the Balance of Ecosystem

Mobile phones were introduced for the convenient communication. Mobile phone subscriptions have grown at very fast pace in the last 20 years. It has penetrated over 70 per cent of the population across the globe. India has also witnessed this growth and has approximately 910 million wireless connections today. Although there are many advantages of mobile phones but it has a negative side also. The effects of electromagnetic (EM) radiations from mobile towers and mobile phone handsets have many adverse effects on health. With increasing number of mobile phones, the number of mobile towers have also increased multifold. The towers installed on the rooftops of houses and in densely populated areas are causing some serious health hazards. On 31 May, 2011, World Health Organization (WHO) confirmed the radiations from the mobile phones as a carcinogenic hazard for human health.

The EMR emitted by the mobile antennas used at the base stations affects the cell structure of the living beings. To meet the demand of higher speed data transfer, we are now using 4G sets, instead of the older mobile sets without internet or with slow speed internet facilities. This is being even much more harmful, for both the flora & fauna, causing immense loss of biodiversity. As we know, any living organism in our mother Earth, has its own unique role in the ecosystem; so loss of anyone will disturb the normal ecological balance, thus ultimately leading to environmental crisis.

Some Evidential Reports

- In Germany, Nordhessen, five school kids: Niklas Binder, Maximilian Görlitz, Jakob Ruckel, Carl-Moritz Köpp and Alexander Popov performed an interesting experiment to know the effect of mobile radio waves on bee population. Behind the idea for the project was the town beekeeper Victor Hernández: He had seen problems developed in a beehive he had, placed near a telephone mast Funkmastes. The five kids decided to try and find out, with his help, whether the mobile phone waves really were affecting the bees. Hernández took a hive to the Schülerforschungszentrum and after a few months of preparation, in June 2016 the experiment was ready to start.

The kids were able to demonstrate a link between mobile phone radiation and bee behaviour. The whole swarm was hooked up to various measuring devices, which monitored different aspects of their daily life: a thermometer measured the temperature, an infrared camera was installed which delivered photos every minute *via* Raspberry-Pi, a photoelectric switch at the entrance monitored the bees' comings and goings and a microphone recorded the volume of the humming. The strength of the mobile radiation was also measured over a long period of time.

Radiation probably causes honey bees (apis mellifera) to partially lose orientation and makes them more aggressive too. Indicators for this included the raised temperature in the hive, decreased movement in and out and louder buzzing. It could have other consequences too.

The young researchers have been recognized publicly too, winning the WWF Galileo Green Youngster Award for their clever experiment. On the 12th of May, 2017, they have received their prize at the Green Tec Awards in Berlin.

- Sparrows were once abundant in the city spaces and rural markets in India. But rising concrete jungles, increasing pollution

> and now, mobile phone towers are causing them to disappear from the Indian landscape, says a group of conservationists in the country. Meanwhile, reports from other parts of the country shows that squirrels also could be victims of increasing mobile phone towers presence and resulting impact of high Electro-Magnetic Radiation.

Ornithologist Amarjit Gupta has pointed out that the number of sparrows across the country has been falling down drastically over a period of time, raising serious concern. According to him, a recent study has shown that sparrows were present only in localities which are located at a particular distance from the towers.

The issue has attracted the attention of Indian authorities in India earlier itself, which forced Ministry of Environment and Forests to constitute an Expert Group to study the possible impacts of communication towers on wildlife, including birds and bees in 2011.

With a wide and deep review of the existing research literature on the issue, the committee found that exposure to Electro Magnetic Radiation at high levels adversely affects living organisms. Later, MoEF has issued an advisory saying that new cell phone towers should not be installed within one kilometre radius of existing ones.

- Villagers and farmers in the Northern parts of the Indian state of Kerala reported on the sudden disappearance of squirrels from the farms and nearby places.

According to George K., a Cocoa farmer in Kannur district, Cocoa cultivators used to face serious annoyance from squirrels during the fruit ripening season. "Cocoa cultivators used to apply pesticides like Furadan, as poison to ward off the issue. But now, they are nowhere seen."

According to him, squirrels are almost absent in these areas now that the ripened Cocoa fruits remain intact, without the need to poisoning. "Though poisoning could have killed many squirrels in the past, we doubt that the increasing presence of mobile phone towers is a reason which has caused the sudden disappearance of the creatures", says he.

Though many conservationists suspect the chances of any particular pesticide used in the farms as a possible cause for the disappearance, they are not ready to rule out the role played by increasing mobile phone tower density in these areas.

- **Dr. Manish Kumar** and **Dr. Rajendra Kumar Singh** of Dr. C.V. Raman University performed an experiment to investigate impact of mobile tower radiation on birds in Durg district both urban and rural areas from January 2018 to May 2018. They recorded and analyzed the data with statistical value obtained from mobile tower impact on birds of different five places of urban and rural area. The urban area has 27 mobile towers and rural area only 6 mobile towers. During the study period they recorded 13 species of both urban and rural area, namely *Bubo bengalensis* [Indian eagle-owl], *Aquila aquila* [Eagle], *Corvus splendence splendence* [Crow], *Acridotheres tristis* [Myna], *Eudynamys melanorhynchus* [Cuckoo, *Koel*], *Columba livia* [Pigeon], *Passer domesticus* [House Sparrow], *Psittacula krameri* [Parrot], *Coracias benghalensis* [Indian Roller], *Antigone* [*Sarus Crane*], *Luscinia brunnea* [Common nightingale], *Chaetorhynchus papuensis* [Drongo] and *Copsychus fulicatus* [Indian robin]. Results indicate that density of birds has decreased 69 per cent in Durg city area and 31 per cent in Anjora village because increase in number of mobile tower radiation.
- According to some coconut producers and vendors, the installation of mobile and WI-FI towers across Goa has affected their plantations. They claim that the size of the coconut has been shrinking drastically and the water inside the coconut has gone.

Horticulturist, Vivek Rao from Madkai said, "Since the mobile towers have increased, the yield of coconuts has reduced and the water inside the coconut is gone. The problem is that the trees get directly exposed to the beam of radiations because of the height of the tower."

Biological Mechanisms of Causing the Harms to Living Cells

Cell Phone Radiation and Oxidative Stress

Free radicals are a group of highly reactive molecules consisting of unpaired electrons in the outer orbit. Free radicals that are derived from oxygen metabolism are known as reactive oxygen species (ROS). ROS are continuously neutralized by antioxidants present in body tissues. Whenever production of ROS exceeds, the scavenging capacity of antioxidants, it leads to OS. In 1992, researchers found that electromagnetic fields increase free radical activity in cells. Within the last decade, *in vivo* animal studies have shown that OS develops in response to cell phone radiation RF-EMW might disturb ROS metabolism by increasing production of ROS or by decreasing antioxidant enzyme activity. Studies have also demonstrated that antioxidants such as melatonin, caffeic acid phenyl ester, vitamin C and vitamin E prevent oxidative stress or apoptosis caused by RF-EMW in animal tissues.

DNA Strand Break and Apoptosis

The effects of RF-EMW on DNA damage have been reported in various studies in the last decade. Lai and Singh reported an increase in single and double-strand DNA breaks in the brain cells of rats that were exposed for 2 hours to a 2450 MHz field at 0.6-1.2 W/kg. They also found that EMW exposure caused DNA-protein and DNA-DNA crosslinks and increased apoptosis in biological samples from rats.

Lai and Singh demonstrated that treating rats with free radical scavengers blocked the effects of EMW on DNA. This suggests that EMW enhances free radical activity in cells, which in turn leads to DNA damage (single or double stranded DNA breaks). More recently, Paulraj and Behari (2006) reported an increase in single strand DNA breaks in the developing brain cells of rats that were exposed for 35 days to 2.45 and 16.5 GHz fields at 1 and 2.01 W/kg. Nikolova *et al.* (2005) reported a low and transient increase in DNA double strand breaks in mouse embryonic stem cells after acute exposure to a 1.7 GHz field.

Effect on Protein Kinase C and Calcium Homeostasis

PKC is a multi-functional protein kinase and is structurally a group of proteins with at least 10 isoenzymes identified thus far. PKC isoenzymes have been reported to differ in their structure, biochemical properties, tissue distribution, subcellular localization, and substrate specificity. PKC has been involved in the regulation of a variety of cellular events including modulation of receptor functions for major hormones and certain enzymes such as adenylate cyclase and ornithine decarboxylase (in the brain). It also plays key role in mediating cellular responses to extracellular stimuli involved in proliferation, differentiation, apoptosis, and exocytotic release in a number of non-neuronal and sperm cells. The PKC enzyme complex is present in rat seminiferous tubules and leydig cells. PKC modulates ion conductance by phosphorylating membrane proteins such as channels, pumps, and ion exchange proteins.

The activation of this enzyme is thought to be biochemically dependent on Ca^{2+}. In fact, Calcium and cAMP are thought to be the two pivotal regulators of sperm flagellar motility. PKC might also play a crucial role in regulating sperm motility together with cAMP and Ca^{2+}.

Recently, Paulraj *et al.* reported decrease in the activity of PKC in developing rat brains that were exposed to 2.45 GHz of microwaves. The authors reported that the microwave damage was more extensive in the hippocampus, which may cause memory loss. Thus, the PKC enzyme is important in sperm motility, and RF-EMW has been reported to decrease PKC activity. We suggest that RF-EMW can cause declines in sperm motility by affecting PKC. Mobile phone-altered PKC activity has been linked with various types of malignancies.

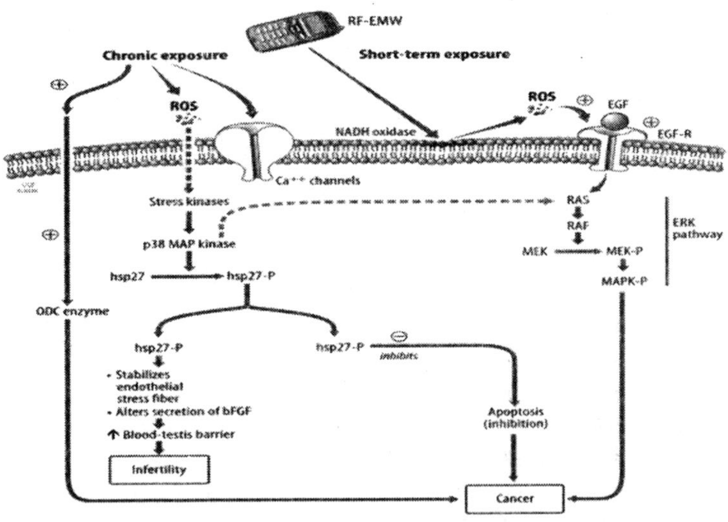

Fig. 15.1: Various Types of Malignancies.

Figure 15.1 shows various cellular targets of radio frequency electromagnetic waves (RF-EMW). Acute (short term) exposure to RF-EMW can stimulate plasma membrane NADH oxidase which can increase reactive oxygen species (ROS) formation. Increase in ROS can stimulate endothelial growth factor (EGF) receptor which in turn activates extra-cellular signal regulated kinase (ERK) pathway. ERK pathway consist of subsequent activation of Ras, Raf proteins and mitogen-activated protein kinase (MAPK). MAPK pathway has tumour promoting role. Chronic exposure to ROS can activate various stress kinase (p. 38, MAP kinase). Activation of p38 MAP kinase can stimulate ERK pathway and also lead to phosphorylation of heat shock proteins (Hsp) which inhibits apoptosis. Inhibition of apoptosis might promote carcinogenesis by prolonging survival of cell with damaged DNA. Hsp also stabilizes endothelial stress fiber and alters secretion of bFGF. This can lead to increase in permeability of blood testis barrier and causes infertility. RF-EMW can also promote cancer by stimulating ornithine decarboxylase (ODC), a rate limiting enzyme in polyamine synthesis pathway as well as by interfering with plasma membrane calcium channels.

Can 5G Be Our Future ?

On 5 November, 2018, Erin Elizabeth's medical conspiracy blog *Health Nut News* "reported" a seemingly disturbing story out of the Netherlands with the headline "Hundreds of birds dead during 5G experiment in The Hague, The Netherlands".

The first EU 5G Appeal was initially submitted in September 2017 to the European Commission demanding a moratorium on the increase of cell antennas for planned 5G expansion. Concerns over health effects from higher radiation exposure include potential neurological impacts, infertility, and cancer.

5G is the next generation of mobile and wireless communication. It will provide faster speeds (up to 100 times) and higher capacity transmissions to carry the massive amount of data that will be generated from the Internet of Things (IoT), driverless cars, smart cities and towns, drones, and for faster video streaming. There are even plans to provide 5G from space, meaning thousands of satellites to cover every square inch of the earth with wireless radiation.

5G will include the higher millimeter wave frequencies never before used for internet and communication technology. The 5G deployment proposes to add frequencies in the microwave spectrum in the low- (0.6 GHz - 3.7 GHz), mid- (3.7GHz - 24 GHz), and high-band frequencies (24 GHz and higher) for faster communications. "If the telecommunications industry's plans for 5G come to fruition, no person, no animal, no bird, no insect and no plant on Earth will be able to avoid exposure, 24 hours a day, 365 days a year, to levels of RF radiation that are tens to hundreds of times greater than what exists today, without any possibility of escape anywhere on the planet. These 5G plans threaten to provoke serious, irreversible effects on humans and permanent damage to all of the Earth's ecosystems."

5G will massively increase the microwave and millimeter wave radiation in our environment, and will have a detrimental effect on wildlife and trees. **5G will substantially increase exposure to radio-frequency electromagnetic fields RF-EMF that has already been proven to be harmful for humans, animals and the environment.**

Risks from 5G include:

- Damage to the eyes — cataracts, retinal damage
- Severe sweating
- Skin damage
- Immune system disruption
- Metabolic disruption
- Neurological disturbance
- Leakage of blood brain barrier
- Damage to sperm
- Increased risk of cancers
- Collapse of insect populations, the base of food for birds and bats
- Rise in bacterial resistance and bacterial shifts
- Damage to plants and trees.

Conclusion

Although mobile telephony has been proved as an indispensable part of our everyday life, and it has made us much more globalized, but the negative effects on living beings (which includes ourselves too) cannot be denied at all. Overall, mobile telephony is destroying the living world surrounding us, slowly but steadily, and it is absolutely alarming for us, the human beings, as we do also belong to this biota. Knowingly or unknowingly, killing them means enhancing the chances of our own living status, at a higher risk.

This is the high time that we should be aware of the restricted use of mobile phones. **It must be Used, but not Misused.** Therefore, we must try to restrict ourselves, regarding the use of such high frequency radiations, as much as feasible.

REFERENCES

Hardell, L., Sage, C., "Biological Effects from Electromagnetic Field Exposure and Public Exposure Standards", *Biomed Pharmacother*, 2008, 62: 104-109.

Kumar, N.R., Sangwan, S., Badotra, P., "Exposure to Cell Phone Radiations Produces Biochemical Changes in Worker Honey Bees", *Toxicol Int.*, 2011, 18(1): 70-72.

Lai, H., Singh, N.P., "Single- and Double-strand DNA Breaks in Rat Brain Cells after Acute Exposure to Radiofrequency Electromagnetic Radiation", *Int. J Radiat Biol.*, 1996, 69: 513-521.

Makker, K., Varghese, A., Desai, N.R., Mouradi, R., Agarwal, A., "Cell Phones: Modern Man's Nemesis?", *Reprod Biomed Online*, 2009, 18: 148-157.

Manish Kumar and Rajendra Kumar Singh, "Effect of Mobile Tower Radiation on Birds: Rural & Urban Area of Durg District (C.G.)", *World Journal of Pharmacy & Pharmaceutical Sciences*, 7(6), June 2018.

Otieno, M.A., Kensler, T.W., "A Role for Protein Kinase C-delta in the Regulation of Ornithine Decarboxylase Expression by Oxidative Stress", *Cancer Res.*, 2000, 60: 4391-4396.

Sukhdeep Kaur, Jaipreet Kaur and Manjit Sandhu, "Effects of Mobile Radiations and its Prevention", *International Journal of Computer Science and Mobile Computing*, Vol. 5, Issue 2, February 2016, pp. 298-304.

World Health Organization (WHO), *WHO Research Agenda for Radio Frequency Fields*, 2006.

Zahid Naeem, "Health Risks Associated with Mobile Phones Use", *International Journal of Health Sciences*, October 2014, 8(4).

16

Globalization and Climate Change
A Case Study of Sundarbans

Priyaranjan Sarkar

Sundarbans is the world's largest contiguous mangrove forest and is one of the natural wonders of the world. It was recognized by UNESCO as a Natural Landscape World Heritage site in 1987. The morpho dynamic of "forest-beauty" Sundarbans with endless diversity of vibrating nature is a suitable habitat of world famous luxuriant mangroves and Royal Bengal Tiger. The Sundarban eco-region formed by the Rivers Ganga, Meghna and Brahmaputra is the tidally active lower part of the largest delta in the world consisting of a warren of rivers, creeks, marshes and alluvial floodplain. Morphological zones of this lower part of the delta are the Ganga tidal plain (West) between rivers Hughli and Baleswar, the Ganga tidal plain (East) between rivers Baleswar and Tetulia, and the Meghna deltaic plain stretching from river Tetulia until Chittagong coastal plain. At the confluence of the delta and the Bay of Bengal, is the single largest mangrove patch of the world spread across about 10,300 sq.km. of which about 60 per cent is in Bangladesh and the rest in India. This mangrove patch is acknowledged worldwide for its outstanding biodiversity, including the Bengal Tiger, and designated as World Heritage Site in both the countries. This littoral mangrove forest besides serving as the habitat for about 200 tigers, accounting for five per cent of the global population in the wild, also imparts protection from storm surges caused by tropical cyclones by attenuating the impact of cyclones that recur on sub-decadal time scales in the Bay of Bengal.[1]

In the words of Anthony Giddens, globalization is defined as "the intensification of worldwide social relations which link distant localities in such a way that local happenings are shaped by events occurring many miles away and *vice versa*." In other words, globalization is the concept and process of developing interconnections beyond borders. Again, Globalization means market-driven supply and demand forces being predominant over need. These interconnections are broadly divided into economic, political and cultural dimensions. Globalization is the "flow" of economic, political and cultural aspects, thus transforming our identities from one of local/national to global. Some scholars assert that globalization is the product of modernity, while others emphasize that economies, governments and people become modern due to globalization. However, whether globalization is good or bad is debatable, but surely it has its own implications on society.

The Inter-governmental Panel on Climate Change (IPCC) defines global climate change or "global warming" as "a change of climate which is attributed directly or indirectly to human activity." Such human activities may be the result of capitalism, individualism and neo-liberalism, modernity, pride for localism/nationalism, neo-realism and utilitarianism (political dimension) and science itself. Post-industrialization modern society did not consider "Nature" as an integral part of our lives. *Laissez faire* capitalism, deregulatory economic policies, the emergence of violent wars in the 20th century and an increase in trade practices are all responsible for global climate change. A post-modern society focused on cooperation and as consequence globalization of scientific culture intensified. Global scientific research and advancements have created a global consciousness about greenhouse gas emissions and climate change. Ironically, the developed West has contributed to carbon emissions for decades which will not be affected much due to climate change but the Global South countries will have to face the consequences of climate change. The Sundarbans is an innocent victim of accelerating global warming and climate change and faces a direct threat to its very existence.[2]

In the past 25 years, sea level has risen at a rate almost double the global average. This is due to a combination of factors including land subsistence patterns. Due to continuous submergence in higher water, as an implication of rise of sea level, the plants are being noted to be shorter and narrower with fewer branches and leaves resulting in lower rates of photosynthesis and regeneration of the mangroves. The sea level rise is also affecting the availability of sediment.[3]

Apart from the human-animal conflict faced by the population dependent on the forest resources for their livelihood, the region is living under the threat of another reality — climate change. As

Sundarbans is a low-lying region and extremely prone to cyclones, climate change significantly impacts the region's flora, fauna and its population.[4]

On the other hand, the islanders, whom the aforementioned section would probably wish to banish to some invisible territory, view what they term as 'weather change' through the lens of their daily chores and what affects their livelihood. Fishers would cite turbulent weather at unlikely times in the year, the farmers cite uncertain rainfall periodicity and frequencies, women are concerned about the rise in water levels during high tides which inundate their homestead ponds with saltwater. The meteorological office forwards the argument of increase in localized weather patterns. The debate on climate has been high on the agenda ever since cyclone Aila and the resultant attention of the outsiders of which even the women in the remotest islands are aware.[5]

Due to climate change, the Sundarbans faces several challenges. With rising sea levels, islands are disappearing and the increasing salinity in the water and soil has severely threatened the health of mangrove forests and the quality of soil and crops. Additionally, there have been serious disturbances to hydrological parameters and change in fishing patterns, resulting in disastrous consequences for fishermen. Frequent cyclones and erratic monsoon raining pattern are damaging ecology and humanity.[6]

In addition to general environment protection laws, India has also set up institutes at both the Central and State levels to specifically tackle the effects of climate change on Sundarbans. However, split responsibilities between Central and States and multitude of institutions has resulted in overlap of responsibilities, loss of time and resources, which makes the institutions ineffective.

With risk of Sundarbans submerging, there is an urgent need for global reduction of emissions and replacement of fossil fuels with renewable energy. Governments also need to promote plantation of local saline resistant seeds. Even as the State and Central Government of India finalize action plans to tackle the problems of climate change take steps for poverty alleviation in one of the world's poorest regions, there is a pressing requirement to set up flood relief centres and rapid action response teams to cyclones and storms.[7]

The Sundarbans has always been a land of natural resource based livelihoods without the option of industrial development, limiting the choices for the local population. The complex interplay of climatic changes along with changing market forces and globalization has led to growing livelihood uncertainties in the Sundarbans in last two decades. The islanders of the Sundarbans have to face both visible and not-so-visible uncertainties in their traditional livelihoods like agriculture and fishing. The immediate uncertainty of a visible and sudden climatic shock, such as flood or cyclone (a frequent occurrence in the Sundarbans), is often a sudden rise in the water level and a related breaching of earthen embankments, inundation of homesteads and agricultural land and salinity intrusion in land and water. As a result, significant loss in the agriculture production and in fish-catch has to be faced by the islander which leads to household food insecurity and economic instability of the islanders, this results in migration of men, mostly to neighbouring states such as Kerala for alternative employment. Consequently, women-headed households are emerging where women have to take care of the supplemental livelihoods, household chores and child care. Women are more likely to become part of the marginal workforce as unskilled labour in the handicraft sector and risky options like crab catching.[8]

Climate change impacts on the health of the people of the Sundarbans in two ways, with the children being more affected by both. First is the rise in water and vector borne diseases after each episode of flooding. Second, these episodes also affect the health care infrastructure making an already weak system more inaccessible, thus depriving the affected islanders of quality-assured medical attention. The impact of climate change on health has not been visible until now. However, the impacts are slowly being shown by the social determinants of health such as poverty, water and sanitation, food production systems and socio-cultural patterns of the society.

In semi-structured interviews with 60 households, almost 44 households out of the 60 have stated that they are forced to take alternative livelihood options just to sustain their families due to the increasing frequency of the climatic adversities. This includes leaving the comfort of traditional livelihoods like agriculture and fishing to take up mostly unskilled option like wage labour, embroidery work, crab collection and migration out of the area. The respondents clearly stated that it is quite difficult for them to cope with this livelihood transition as, firstly, they do not have required skills to catch up with new kind of livelihood options and, secondly, there are very few options available in the Sundarbans. Hence, migration is often the most feasible way out.[9]

Warming up of the Earth's surface is changing the monsoon and cyclone patterns in South Asian countries. Countries like India and

Bangladesh are frequently facing severe cyclonic storms leading to severe damage to the coastal areas of these countries. The Sundarbans on the eastern coastal areas of West Bengal in India and the western coastal areas of Bangladesh is a contiguous chain of mangrove trees which play an important role in preventing the inland areas from severe damage due to coastal erosion, tidal onslaughts and natural calamities. However, the mangrove forests are dying and animals living there are becoming endangered or completely extinct.[10]

The Sundarbans are the world's largest mangrove forest and is the home of a large number of flora and fauna including the "Royal Bengal Tiger". Illegal clearance of forests, digging fishing ponds and digging for oil, lumbering and collecting honey commercially are destroying the natural habitat. The great inflow of foreign tourists has increased employment as well as recognition of the forest at the international sphere. However, unregulated use of boats from Calcutta to Dhaka to carry tourists has caused oil spills. Tourism has also generated litter, posing serious threats to the ecological habitat. Many small islands are on the verge of sinking due to rising sea levels. Clearance of mangrove trees to create "mangrove pathways" for tourists have left stretches of mangrove vegetation reduced to greyish landscape of sediments where tree stumps stick out like dead sticks.[11]

The level of literacy and education is very low in the small villages of Sundarbans which has led to lack of social security, informalization of employment and migration of residents (especially male) to other cities or states in search of jobs. Therefore, the residents resort to dangerous activities in the forest at the expense of their lives. Digging of ponds and opening a channel to the sea will increase the salinity of the soil and make it unfit for farming. In the year 2012, the proposed Rampal Thermal Power Project, a joint initiative by the Governments of India and Bangladesh posed serious threats to the ecology of Sundarbans. Civil society organizations and environmentalists both from inside and outside the countries protested against the draconian project. UNESCO and International Union for Conservation of Nature (IUCN) expressed ugly thoughts about the coal-fired project within 4 kms of ecologically critical area (ECA) of the Sundarbans. The power plant also threatens to displace over 3500 land-owning families and other dependents on the forest for life. Despite strong resistance, the project continues to work.

Shrimp cultivation in Sundarban has become a lucrative means of livelihood. Due to the high salinity of soil and frequent storms, flood cultivation is a hardy task in Sundarbans. Thus, people have shifted to shrimp cultivation as an alternative because it appeared to be paying more than agriculture. Shrimp cultivation is, however, harmful for the environment of Sundarbans. Shrimp cultivation erodes the mud dykes that prevents entry of saline water inland, also constant treading of mangrove roots in search of shrimp seedlings destroys the trees. Faulty collection of shrimps from the sea also disrupts the aquatic fish population of the delta.

Demand for crabs from other Asian countries like Japan, Malaysia, China, Thailand, Singapore, Taiwan and South Korea have shifted employment of some from shrimp to crabs. The global demand has provided a transnational dimension to the popularity of Sundarbans. Crab cultivation is more environment friendly than shrimps, but this new source of income depends on international demand, and bitter diplomatic relations with these countries can worsen the trade practices.

Climate change is not limited to the local. Carbon emissions in the distant West affect climate everywhere. Neo-liberalization and globalization policies have allowed unchecked emissions into the atmosphere and have made coastal ecology fragile and vulnerable. Rising temperatures of the earth's surface will force coastal populations to migrate due to climate crisis.

International Relations Theory having been dominated by neo-realism recognizes an anarchic international sphere which cannot be governed by global governance. Yet, in the view of neo-realists this is true. International cooperation for climate change policies undertaken by the UN Framework Convention on Climate Change lacks authority necessary for implementation, monitoring and enforcement of policies in every member country. A recommendation by the IUCN to add Sundarbans in the list of World Heritage Sites in Danger due to the Rampal Thermal Power Project was refused by UNESCO chaired by China because of Indo-China geopolitical relations in the region.

Ecological modernization is a theory that promotes emission trading and tax breaks for renewable resource industries and technologies. However, it may stand against national ecological standards. International trade is beneficial for countries with higher comparative advantages. It leads to growth and development of economies. Economic, political and cultural globalization has brought South Asian countries to the global market. Thus, deglobalizing the existing structure can exacerbate the ecological balance of nature. Therefore, rather than deglobalizing, governments should decentralize powers to local sustainable governments to reduce emissions locally, reform the economic structure through ecological modernization and cooperate with other governments at an international sphere to reduce climate change.[12]

NOTES

1. O'Malley, L.S.S., *Bengal District Gazetteers 24 Pgs*, W.B. District Gazetteers, Department of Higher Education, Government of West Bengal, Calcutta, 1998.
2. Malone, E.L. (2002). "Hot Topics: Globalization and Climate Change", *Social Thought and Research*, pp. 143-45.
3. Sanyal, P., 1999. "Sundarbans — The Largest Mangrove Diversity on the Earth", K.R. (eds.), *Naya Prakash*, Calcutta, India, pp. 427-28.
4. Chaudhuri, A.B. and Choudhury, A., "Mangroves of the Sundarban", *India IUCN*, Vol. I, Bangkok, p. 247.
5. Mahadevia, K. and M. Vikas, 2012. "Climate Change — Impact on Sundarbans: A Case Study", *Journal of Environmental Science*, 2(1). Online at: *http://environmental.scientific-journal.com*/articles/2/1.pdf (Viewed on November 21, 2020).
6. Hazra, S., Samanta, K., Mukhopadhyay, A. and Akhand, A. (2010), *Temporal Change Detection (2001-2008) Study of Sundarban*, Kolkata: School of Oceanographic Studies, Jadavpur University.
7. Government of West Bengal (2010). *West Bengal State Action on Climate Change*, Kolkata: Government of West Bengal.
8. Mahadevia, K. and M. Vikas (2012). *Ibid.*
9. Loucks, C., S. Barber-Meyer, M. Hossain, A. Barlow, and R. Chowdhury (2010). "Sea Level Rise and Tigers: Predicted Impacts to Bangladesh's Sundarban Mangroves", *Climatic Change*, 98(1-2), pp. 291-92.
10. Khalil, G.M. (1992). "Cyclones and Storm Surges in Bangladesh: Some Mitigative Measures", *Natural Hazards*, 6(1), p. 11.
11. Chaudhuri, A.B. and Choudhury, A., *Ibid.*, p. 251.
12. Malone, E.L. (2002). *Ibid.*, pp. 168-73.

17

Specific Indian Films Based on Global Environmental Issues

Impact on Human Life

Nandini Chakraborty

Introduction

The role of Indian media in promoting environment and sustainability concerns the Indian films have played a revolutionary role in building nationalism and endorsing pro-developmental values; and it continues to be powerfully positioned to do so. Films on environment and wildlife have come a long way in India in the last decade. Celluloid seems to be quite a medium of choice to take the message across. The film making format has also seen a change with many film makers changing over to new ways of storytelling.

To promote conservation of bio-diversity and build environmental awareness, Bollywood films can play a big role. If there is little bit of an attempt from mainstream cinema like Bollywood to present issues on environment and wildlife, then it will help us to reach more audiences. Bollywood films should build environmental awareness. Visual media is now recognized as one of the most powerful, engaging and emotive ways to sensitize audiences towards the cause of environmental conservationism. Films illustrate the sheer beauty of the natural world, inspiring an entire generation of conservationists across the globe.

It is not necessary that all such films need to be hard-hitting and serious. Film industry can even make nature films for the masses with pure entertainment value, with a message; save the earth. If more people are able to relate to nature and environment through an entertaining film, even then the purpose is served. Pointing out that Indian documentary makers like Mike Pandey have been successful in promoting the cause through his films; but India needs more such efforts. Documenting the massacre of whale sharks on the Indian coast, *Shores of Silence*, made in 2000 by Pandey, became a landmark film after it was successful in moving the Indian government into bringing in legislation and ban the killing of whale sharks.

Safeguarding the environment is one of the major challenges faced by most of the major countries in the world. Though there are numerous laws drafted by the government in this regard, it lags in the efficient implementation of it. It is high time that government has to chalk out the plan to educate a common man about the implications of deteriorating environment and his/her role in safeguarding it.

When it comes to the role of visual media, it can be discerned that it is below partaking consideration of the influence it has towards the masses. Media have to make the comprehensive coverage of environmental issues which would help in preaching the common man on his/her role in building the cleaner environment with due responsibility.

Objective of the Study

The objective of the study is to estimate the extent of the role of visual media on the management of environmental issues: their cause and effect on human life. Also it is to analyze their performance, in effective, in other words the most likely way they have improved speedy: efficient, effective, and qualitative methods of environmental awareness. It is hoped that this study will give an insight into the effectiveness of the mass media as well as visual media in environmental issues and its impact on human life.

Review of Literature

A research by Archibald, Erika Francesca (1996), on how environmental reporters on daily newspapers construct news of the environment, made an exploratory analysis on daily newspaper reporters who cover the environmental beat, in order to learn how they operate and how they make certain crucial decisions. Long interviews were conducted with twenty environmental reporters from daily newspapers throughout the United States. They said environmental topics generally took more time to do than other news stories. Problems these reporters faced included not enough time or space to understand, cover and write about these multi-level, subtle and often uncertain issues, and dealing with editors who have little interest in the environment and non-traditional news stories.

Craig Trumbo (1996) on "Constructing climate change": claims and frames in US news coverage of an environmental issue, median empirical content analysis of a decade of coverage of climate change in five national newspapers in the US is presented. The analysis is based on the perspective, drawn from social problems theory, that the content of news discourse can be understood in terms of claims-making and framing. Climate change is also discussed in terms of Downs' issue-attention cycle, a five stage model describing the rise and fall of social attention to important issues. Climate change, as a news story, is described as exhibiting three phases that are related to the sources quoted and the frames presented in the news coverage. Result of the analysis shows that scientists tend to be associated with frames emphasizing problems and causes, while politicians and special interests tend to be associated with frames emphasizing judgments and remedies. Results also show how scientists declined as news sources as the issue became increasingly politicized.

Guedes, O.M.R. (1996), on Green politics, ideology and communication, made a detailed analysis of the Brazilian mass media, looking at how particular views of environmental issues are constructed and maintained by the media. It analyses the production of environmental news through a combination of content analysis, case study and in-depth, semi-structured interviews with journalists to examine the way they see the characteristics of environmental reporting and its process of production.

A study by Randazzo, Ryan C.R. (2001), "Context and bias in environmental journalism" in the leading United States daily newspapers online *vs.* print: A content analysis on newspaper coverage of environmental issues, especially for lacking context and being biased. The development of the Internet has created new opportunities for newspapers to provide better environmental coverage. A content analysis examines what kinds and how much context is provided in environmental articles in five leading U.S. daily newspapers. It also examines how biased those articles are in terms of balancing both sides of controversies. Differences between print and online versions of the newspapers were examined.

A study focusing on the US network television coverage in the 1990s suggests that environmental aspects have been largely absent from non-news entertainment and fictional prime time coverage (McComas *et al.*, 2001). The old newsroom maxim, If it bleeds it leads, still appears to grip many news organizations, despite the fact that most of the crime stories that suck up media attention have very little national relevance. The networks morning shows carry an estimated 69 crime stories for each environmental story they do. The crime-to-environment coverage ratios are also dismal for other outlets: *Cable News*, 9-to-1; *Online News*, 6-to-1; *Evening Network News*, 5-to-1.

Yuki Sampei, Midori Aoyagi-Usui (2009) examined analysed Japanese newspaper coverage of global warming from January 1998 to July 2007 and how public opinion during parts of that period were influenced by newspaper coverage. It show a dramatic increase in newspaper coverage of global warming from January 2007 correlated with an increase in public concern for the issue. Before January 2007, it has found that coverage of global warming had an immediate but short-term influence on public concern. With such transitory high levels of media coverage we suggest that for more effective communication of climate change, strategies aimed at maintaining mass-media coverage of global warming are required.

A study by Daniel Adel (2013) on "Mainstream media's environmental coverage: The sound of silence" examined the report released by Pew Research Center's Project for Excellence in Journalism to review a range of national and local news organizations across platforms from January 2011 to May 2012. The study showed that among 30 national news organizations in the United States, environmental coverage represented just 1.2 per cent of headlines. Meanwhile, entertainment and crime coverage continued to dominate the media space. For some news organizations, entertainment and crime garnered 20 to 60 times more coverage, respectively, than did the environment.

Content Analysis

Visual media is known as the effective means of mass communication, which influence people widely. Over the last 70 years, visual media has transformed our everyday life to the point where we are aware of world events within minutes of their occurrence. World topics, such as the environment and global warming, have progressed in visual media coverage due to new technologies and public interest. Overall, there is more choice, freedom, speed and competition in all aspects of media today.

The coverage of environmental issues has become slightly politicized, which can be associated with many different social, economic and scientific events in the last decade, but the general perspective has been shaped by the techno-centric environmental perspective, which stresses traditional beliefs and values, emphasizing progress, technology, production and materialism. Also the media reinforce the belief that conflicting social values.

From 1960s to 2020s, Bollywood films largely dominated the media industry. This new technology became widely popular at this time. It was at this time that the environment and related terms entered the mass media vocabulary as a way of labelling this new way of looking at humankind-habitat relationships. The popular first film story on natural disaster, in the India was, 1965s *Waqt*. Journalists also began to cover environmental issues early in the 1960, but had to compete with the television and films. The 1960s were a time of political, social, cultural and psychological change. These brought out new movements and changes, which were spread with the help of increased visual media attention. The Bollywood films expanded into a medium able to deliver news shape public opinion and unite people in great moments.

Raising the awareness of a society through media is one of the strategies required for the effective realization of environmental objectives and goals. It is truly crucial to raise public awareness of environmental issues. Visual media is efforts to aware the audience about environmental issues, and the struggle against the environmental problems.

Visual media or Bollywood Films can inspire the mass "To Save the Earth." We cannot escape the impact of our actions have on the environment. Global warming has taken over our lives, tsunamis are striking our coastal areas, floods and droughts have had a major bearing on the availability of clean water, thus, affecting the production of crops and price of food. So, it is high time we, as guardians of the Earth, step up and do our bit to save the environment from impending doom. Many movies have also attempted to warn us about this, by showing us the effects of environmental disasters. They have been entertaining, but these movies have taught us a valuable lesson, that, do not take the Earth for granted.

Here is a list of Indian (Bollywood) films, that showed us the importance of saving the earth, and respecting the factors of nature:

Waqt

An earthquake destroys the home and town of Lala Kedarnath, displacing his family. The movie depicts how a simple natural act of nature can turn your entire life around. Members of a family are separated in a natural disaster. Several years down the line, they are not united but their lives are strangely interconnected.

Mother India

The movie depicts how a storm that causes floods in a village, destroys its harvests. Starvation and disease plague among the villagers, who have to take extreme measures to save their families.

Dasavathaaram

A tsunami strikes the coast, destroying property and claiming lives in its wake. But its biggest boon was the destruction of the bio-weapon created for environmental harm.

Bhopal Express

The movie is based on the Bhopal gas tragedy of 1984. The poisonous gas clouds released from the Union Carbide factory took several lives and impaired many others.

Jal

The movie captures the severe drought in the Rann of Kutch. The story revolved around Bakka, who tries to find water in the desert amidst severe water scarcity.

Tum Mile

The movie is loosely based on the Maharashtra floods of 2005, which affected large areas of Mumbai. Spoiler alert: a guy is electrocuted when he falls in the water with an electric cable.

Kai Po Che

Govind loses all his money when an earthquake strikes his town, destroying his sports shop. To make matters worse, religion and politics intervene in the disaster relief operations, making his life more miserable.

My Name Is Khan

Set in the United States, this movie tells us the story of Rizwan Khan and the struggle of the Muslim community in the 'States' after 9/11. The movie shows parts of Georgia submerged in water due to a massive storm that causes floods.

Lagaan (2001)

Lagaan is one of the most grossing films of Bollywood which portrays the condition of Indians under the British rule and how Indians had to suffer in the times of a drought. The film tells us the story of a village, that was unable to produce any crop due to shortage of water and how the Britishers refused any excuses when they could not pay taxes. We pray for those who lost their lives in natural calamities and we will stand by the survivors for ever.

Kedarnath

Mansoor is in love with a Hindu Brahmin girl and her family is against their relationship. She angrily prays for a disaster, which is followed by a cloudburst, landslides, and floods. As they struggle for their lives, the pilgrim city of Kedarnath faces the wrath of nature.

Conclusion

The way that Bollywood films as well as visual media has portrayed; environmental issues have changed radically in the past few years. Environmental issues often are not considered newsworthy unless something in large scale occurs with a notable impact on everyday life. The films spread an outpouring of awareness came of these natural disasters, their effects, tragedy, and mass media diligently informed audiences of every detail as the following cleanup events unfolded. Most environmental news are not front-page material, but films often made on those untold stories.

The media gets the ultimate say in what is deemed as important. In today's modern times, the green living movement intersects local state and federal politics. It impacts business practices, art and the media, education and health in India. The purpose of green living movement is to control pollution or protect plant and animal diversity. Now-a-days, film media has played in setting perceptions and creating awareness on environmental issues.

In the past decades, sustainability and environmental awareness have gained media attention. Due to increasing media coverage, our society is becoming more aware of the effects that our activities put on the health of the environment. In this regard, the media has a big role to play in making people aware of environment issues.

The growing awareness of the two-way relationship between environmental impact and socio-economic development, and the challenges posed by environmental problems has led to the insight that underlines the needs to strengthen the ways in which existing development programmes address both the causes and effects of problems in each country. The need to spread environmental awareness is enormous in the context of successfully addressing environmental problems. It is linked to environmental education.

In this modern knowledge-society, visual media plays the role of facilitator of development, disseminator of information, and an agent of social change. Both urban and rural people were not well informed about the mode of destruction and protection of the environment. One of the causes of the deep rooted environmental problems in a country is lack of awareness which is at the very heart of the inappropriate management and utilization of environmental resources.

The visual media can identify and bring to a halt forces affecting the natural and even the man-made environment. It matters much how the public mind can be mobilized to reduce pollution and promote environmental quality. The goal should be to focus certain relative aspects leading to environmental protection through conservation emphasizing the protection of earth. It is genuinely expected that the media play quite a significant role in influencing mass-awareness against the excessive use of energy.

REFERENCES

Bandhu, Desh, Dyal, R. (Eds.), *Environmental Education for a Sustainable Future*, Indian Environmental Society, New Delhi, 1999.

Bennett, W.L., *News: The Politics of Illusion*, New York, Longman, 2002.

Boykoff, M. and Mansfield, M., "Ye Olde Hot Aire: Reporting on Human Contributions to Climate Change in the UK Tabloid Press", *Environ. Res.*, 2008, Lett, 3:1-83.

Boykoff, M., "The Cultural Politics of Climate Change Discourse in UK Tabloids", *Polit. Geogr.*, 2008, 27:549-694.

Das, Nandita, *A Study on Social and Environmental Impact of TV and Radio Programmes*, Center of Media Studies, New Delhi, 2001.

Das, R.C., Baral, J.K., Sahu, N.C. and Misras, M.K., *The Environmental Divide —The Dilemma of Developing Countries*, 1998.

McChesney, R.W. Rich, *Media, Poor Democracy: Communication Politics in Dubious Times*, Urbana/Chicago: University Ill. Press, 1998.

McCombs, M., "A Look at Agenda-setting: Past, Present and Future", *Journalism Studies*, 2005, 6: 5.

been organized to reinvent the government. Some questions have been raised in the debate as to whether the state public administration should be people-centric or capital-centric or the nature or size of the state government will change etc. The first satellite connections were made in 1970s. Imperialism neo-colonial ever forced house wives to wear Manchester clothes, cold water has once again poisoned developing countries. But the disorder that infected the world in the 1990s in the name of globalization is its first symptom of rapid international investment system. Multinational corporations continue to play the most important role as carries of this disease.[8] The market oriented government policy adopted by the national and state governments has increased the potential for global market expansion not only this, the former thinking of the [illegible] has also changed. New investment policy, [illegible] policy, technology exchange and consumerist economy, a new world culture has emerged, breaking the barrier of state culture that the revolution has [illegible] in the world of information technology. The first implication of this complex and multifaceted change were the rapid development of technology in the last half of the twentieth century, the idea of electronic government and the consequent results. The revolutionary development of communication and information technology in West Bengal has revolutionized the world market and especially the administration.

Globalization has marked a revolutionary change in the nature and [illegible] of public administration. Public administration has been forced [illegible] [illegible] and resulting. Good [illegible] have [illegible] of West [illegible] efficient management and rapid development management. The E-Governance or IT-based governance process has not [illegible] in the West Bengal administration [illegible]. E-Governance is the use of information technology in government activities to achieve the goals of the organization's authority. There has been talk of SMART governance in this information-based governance process. The feature of SMART GOVERNANCE is — S = Simple, M = Moral, A = Accountable, R = Responsive and T = Transparent. These are just some of the goal setting share-ware that you can use — 1. Exchange of information between citizen, government departments and business groups. 2. Recognize speed and efficiency in the delivery of government services. 3. Improving internal skills. 4. Decrease in expenditure and increase in revenue. 5. Restructuring in the administrative process. 6. Development of quality of services.

INDEX